Thoughts for Life's Journey

George Matheson

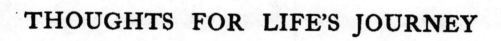

THOUGHTS FOR LIFE'S JOURNEY

P. 64   A mother's love for the child

THOUGHTS FOR LIFE'S JOURNEY

BY
GEORGE MATHESON
D.D., LL.D., F.R.S.E.

AUTHOR OF
"LEAVES FOR QUIET HOURS"
"WORDS BY THE WAYSIDE" ETC

LONDON
JAMES CLARKE & CO
13 & 14 FLEET STREET
1907

PREFATORY NOTE

IN accordance with a suggestion made by the publishers to the author some few months before his death, these devotional sermonettes, which have appeared from time to time in *The Christian World,* are now issued in collective form. Eighty-six sermonettes are here included, dealing with varied subjects that may appeal to varied minds. In the course of their previous issue the author received much eloquent testimony regarding the help and comfort derived from their perusal, which fact would tend to the belief that this further offering in a more permanent form is not without some measure of justification.

THOUGHTS FOR LIFE'S JOURNEY

THE HOUR OF GOD'S CALL

"The Master is come, and calleth for thee."—JOHN XI. 28.

IT was a strange time for Martha to get a call —just when her own special gift had come to a stand. There was no further room for her practicalness; she had been forced to fold her hands. The power to work had ended; the necessity to wait had come. It was a time when Martha might well have said to herself: "I have no longer any calling; my occupation is gone now. There are no more tables to serve, no more friends to entertain, no more hospitalities to dispense, no more sick brothers to nurse, not even any more funeral arrangements to make; my work is done." Yet it was at that hour the call came. It was at the close of her own day that God's day *began* for

7

her. It was in the stillness of all her special powers that the knocker struck the door.

And I think, my brother, it is ever so that thy Father deals with thee. I do not think He knocks at the door of thy special gift; rather, it seems to me, does He seek thy neglected door. He would bring thee out precisely by that gate which was not thine entrance gate. Why does He so often block that particular way on which thou art going? "To teach thee distrust of *thyself*," cry a hundred voices. Nay, to teach thee to trust thyself in more directions. Why should all thy work be special! Is there to be no road between thee and thy brother—no sympathy with that which is *another's* endowment? Why has God stripped thee of thy power of active service? To teach thee thine impotence? No, to show thee thy power on the other side of the hill. Is there no service but action! Is there no blessing for Mary! Is there no work for those who can only stand and wait, only lie and wait! What of that wondrous movement which makes no noise—the surrender of the will! What of those who suffer and pine not, endure and complain not, bear and doubt not! How *came* they to that blissful call? Through the shadows of the evening. They once were like thee—believing in nothing but the hand. God hid

The Hour of God's Call

the garish day, and the hand grew powerless. And then the Master called through another avenue—a slighted avenue; and the inward will arose and said, "I have found a neglected door."

Find the slighted avenue .... the neglected door.

THE OPEN EFFECT OF SECRET ASPIRATION

"Pray to thy Father which is in secret; and thy Father which seeth in secret shall reward thee openly."—MATT. VI. 6.

THE doctrine of Jesus differs here from the view of the moderns. The common voice of *our* day is, " Pray in secret, and thy Father will reward thee *secretly*." I am told that the only use of prayer is to calm the *mind*—to breath *within* me a spirit of peace. And truly, even if that were all, it would be a most valuable boon. But it would not be an " *open* reward." It would be a thing as latent as my prayer. It would be a little secret of the heart between me and my Father. Its coming would be unknown to the world; its presence would be unseen by the world; its music would be unheard by the world. That may be very sublime, but it is not what Christ promised. What He says is that the prayer is to be secret, but the reward open. The prayer is to be unwitnessed; the answer is to be public. The prayer is to be veiled; the answer is to be read of all men. The prayer is to be within closed doors; the answer is to be in the wide wide world.

My brother, do not say that the purpose of your prayer is to calm your mind! That is not an end; it is a beginning. If you have a calm mind you will come out into the open. Your Father's aim is not that you should enter into rest; it is that you should enter into movement. He offers you His peace, not to make you lie down in green pastures, but to make you walk in the paths of righteousness. It is not the secrecy of our prayer that He values; it is the publicity which the secret hour kindles. Tell me! have not our most public moments come from our most secret hours? When you were a child you built castles in the air. They were rather castles in the heart; they were all inside—within the closed doors of the soul. These castle-buildings were your first prayers. They were the golden wishes of your spirit, and they were only visible to you and your Father. There was no axe or hammer heard when these houses were building; they were prayers to your Father "in secret." Yet these prayers have had an open reward. You are *richer* to-day by reason of the castles you built in your heart. I do not say your life has ever reached the measure of them; I know it has not. But I do say it has reached more than it would have reached without them. Your love's young dream has kept you from the miry clay. Your vision of the hill has nerved you for the plain. In the secret places of your heart you have heard distant music—the world would say imaginary music. But it is to this secret music that the march of your outward life has been timed. It is this far-off melody that has fired you for the actual battle. It is this song in the night that has made you conqueror in the day. Build, my brother, your castles of prayer—build on ! They will meet you again in stone and lime. You will find them in the daylight world—the world of life and action. Your poetry will help your prose; your flight will aid your walking. Stand in the secret place of golden wishes ; but know assuredly that there is nothing secret which shall not be revealed !

THE CLEANSING OF THE TEMPLE

" When He had made a scourge of small cords, He drove them all out of the temple, and the sheep, and the oxen ; and poured out the changers' money, and overthrew the tables ; and said, Make not my Father's house an house of merchandise."— JOHN II. 15, 16.

WE all begin by making the house of God a house of merchandise. When people begin to think seriously, religion first presents itself as a present penance for the sake of future gain. A man says : " I am told pious people get on in the world ; God blesses them in their basket and in their store. True, church is very dull ; but church means a blessing in life. If I serve God, God will smile on me. If I seek Him on Sunday, He will not forget me in the struggle for bread on Monday." That is what Christ calls buying and selling in the temple of God. You offer the Almighty a sight of your grave face on the chance that He will pay you back by a gift of sumptuous living. For a time the Lord suffers this. He lets you for a space bring your merchandise into the temple, for it is better to come to the temple with

13

your merchandise than not to come at all. But by-and-by He feels that the time for expulsion has arrived. He takes a scourge of small cords and drives out the sheep and oxen. What is that scourge? It is a form of experience. What is it that drives out the mercantile view of religion? It is just the discovery that the good are *not* physically rewarded. Nothing drives out the merchandise from the temple like the experience of Job. We see him leading a good life; yet we see the sheep and oxen taken from him just as they are taken from bad people. It is meant to show him, it is meant to show us, that religion is not a mercantile transaction, that the rewards of God are not sheep and oxen. To every growing spirit the voice of Christ is this: " Make not My Father's house a house of merchandise ! "

Lord, I understand Thy dealings in the great Temple. Often have I wondered why the white robes of fortune were not reserved for the whitest souls. I do not wonder now. I understand why it is written of Thy coming glory, "Of that day and that hour knoweth no man." If we did know, we should crowd Thy temple as we crowd the market-place—for gain. We should go up to Thy house in multitudes, we should jostle one another to get first in ; there would be a struggle for the

Religion is not a mercantile Transaction

survival of the fittest. But the fittest would be the most selfish; it would be a struggle for the glory of the flesh; we should seek, not the prodigal's penitence, but the prodigal's ring. Therefore it is that in the far country Thou revealest not the ring. Thou *hidest* the music and the dancing that await us in Thy house. Thou comest to meet us *without* the costly robe, with only the song of welcome. Often with a scourge of small cords Thou drivest the sheep and oxen from our temple. Often in the very front of our altar Thou overturnest the table of our gains. Men say, "If He loved them, would He overturn their table?" It is because of Thy love, O Lord! Thou preparest for me a table in the wilderness, lest I should seek Thee, not for love, but for gold. Thou makest me sit down in the presence of mine enemies, lest I should come to Thee for the winning of earthly friends. Thou leadest me through the valley of the shadow of death, lest I should be comforted by any rod and staff but Thine. Cleanse from merchandise the temple of my soul!

THE TOUCH OF JESUS

"Jesus put forth His hand, and touched the leper, saying, I will; be thou clean."—MATT. VIII. 3.

Do you think that in the view of St. Matthew the touch had anything to do with the miracle? It seems to me that we are under a delusion on this point. I have heard it said that Christ never worked without human means. It is true that He always brought Himself into contact with the afflicted party. But I do not think the motive of the contact was the use of human means. I believe the contact was in every case something over and above the miracle. It was quite possible to have healed this leper by a word alone. It would be quite possible for God Almighty to say to all the moral lepers of the world, "Be thou clean!" and the cure would be Divinely perfect. Why, then, does He not? Just because the cure would be Divinely perfect. God wants it to be humanly perfect, and this can only be effected by a touch. Elijah in the desert may be fed by ravens or he may be fed by man's philanthropy.

16

The Touch of Jesus

The physical effect will be the same, but not the moral effect. Elijah fed by the ravens is not a whit nearer to his kind than Elijah faint and hungry; but Elijah fed by human hands becomes himself more human. The greatest calamity of a leper was not his leprosy; it was his divorce from his fellow-man. It was not his physical disease that divorced him; it was the belief in his moral contagion. His greatest cry was for some one to touch him—to bridge the river of separation. It was easy to get the touch after he was healed. But the hard thing was to get contact before healing—to receive the touch before receiving the mandate, " Be thou clean ! " His fellow-men would not grant him that boon. Doubtless they prayed for his recovery, but they would not touch him *un*-recovered. God could have healed him in answer to their *prayers*, but He wanted to heal him in answer to their contact.

Jesus, Thou alone hast touched the leper un-healed. I have read of a woman who touched the hem of Thy garment; we call it the touch of faith. But Thou hast a touch for the hem of *our* garment, and this is also a touch of faith. It is a touching of that which is still impure, and it is prompted by a faith in my possibilities. It is a hand put out to give me a chance—a hand

B

preceding the voice—preceding the cure. Thy touch lingers not for the cleansing of my leprosy. It seeks me in the dark and in the cold. It is a touch of faith, not of sight. Thou comest to me when I am still in the shadow. It is on a *soiled* finger Thou puttest the adoption ring; it is on a broken body Thou layest the best robe. Thou comest to me before my dawn, when, as yet, there is nothing to see. Thy coming is a walk by faith. Thou takest me on trust ere I have done anything. Just as I am, without one plea, Thou touchest me—Thou layest on me Thine ordaining hand. Just as I am, unhealed, uncleansed, Thou touchest the hem of my soiled garment, and Thy voice says to my soul, "Take another chance; come and try once more!" O Jesus, great is Thy faith!

THE THINGS INDESTRUCTIBLE

"Abideth faith, hope, love, these three."—1 Cor. XIII. 13.

AND so there are three things which are never to die, which I am to carry with me beyond the grave! Three pearls are to be saved from the wreck of time and landed on the shore! Two of the preservations surprise me. I could never wonder at the immortality of love, for heaven without love would be the world without the sun. But faith and hope—where is the place for *these* in heaven! I thought faith would drop her wings when she lighted on the soil of home; I thought hope would draw in her sails when she touched fruition's shore. The men of old time told me that all mystery would vanish when the curtain of death infolded me. They told me that faith would be lost in sight, that hope would fade in fulfilment. Paul says they shall *abide*. How shall they abide with perfect revelation? How shall faith breathe in the cloudless sky; how shall hope flutter in the windless air? If these abide, shadow must abide; and why is shadow there? Why prolong the

19   B 2

winter of my faith and the spring-time of my hope when the summer of my love has come?

In the *interest* of that love, O my soul. Hast thou considered the place of the shadows! Are they not the very pinions of thy love! Is not thy pity ever born of danger! It would die if it saw clearly. Perfect morning would scatter the fairest of the gems. It would destroy the need of thy charity. It would lame the feet of thy sympathy. It would clip the wings of thy compassion. It would close the gates of thy solicitude for others. It would end the days of thine unselfish prayers. Keep thy shadows, O my soul! Keep a little rim of darkness round thy sun! Keep a spot unrevealed in the dealings of thy God! Keep in the new world a place for the cross of Jesus— a place where love may see the cloud and feel a brother's pain! Thy perfect sight would be dearly purchased by the loss of thy Lord's passion. The cloud that covers the transfigured glory is itself a glory. If thou wouldst give rein to thy love, leave in the Paradise of God a margin for faith and hope.

THE PURPOSE OF GOD'S LEADING

" He leadeth me in the paths of righteousness—for His name's sake."—Ps. XXIII. 3.

WE hear a great deal about the leading of God; but I think there is no subject on which we have such confused ideas. We say that God's is an *individual* Providence. On the faith of that, we ask for some trinket, ring, or gewgaw. We do not get it. Then we say, " It is all a delusion; God cares nothing for individuals!" The Psalmist has avoided this confusion. On the one hand, he has no doubt whatever of an individual Providence. Every note of the Psalm is personal : " The Lord is *my* shepherd," "He leadeth *me*." But on the other hand, he recognises that the leading itself is not for an individual *end:* "He leadeth me in the path of righteousness—He leadeth me for His name's sake." This is very strange language. We should have expected him to say, " God is leading me in green pastures on account of the good life *I* have led." On the contrary, he says " God is leading me in green pastures to further the good

21

of other people—to minister to those who have *not* led a good life." And I think the experience of the Psalmist will be found true to all experience. I do not believe that any man is led into prosperity or into adversity for the *sake* of that prosperity or adversity; it is always for the sake of God's name or holiness. You pray for worldly wealth and it comes to you. Has God led you into that wealth? Yes, but not to reward your prayer. Rather would I say that the prayer and the riches are both parts of His guidance into a path of humanitarian righteousness where you can minister to the sorrows of man. Why was Abraham promised the land of Canaan? As a reward for leaving Ur of the Chaldees? No, but with the view of making blessed all the families of the earth. God did not give him the new country as a recompense for leaving the old; He inspired him to leave the old because He meant to give him the new.

Lord, lead me to green pastures for Thy *name*'s sake! Thy name is Love; lead me to green pastures for the *sake* of love! I do not seek the verdant spot that I may rest there, but that through my rest another may be helped in toil. I ask the gifts of fortune, not that I may keep them, but that I may share them. If my pastures be green let me feed Thy flock; if my waters be quiet

let me launch ships for *Thee!* Often in the days
of youth I have prayed that Thou wouldst lead me
to the New Jerusalem whose streets are paved
with gold. I would not unqualifiedly pray for
that now. I should like to make a condition—
that I should not be forced always to remain there.
I should like to have the egress, as well as the
ingress, of the city of gold. I should like freedom
to *transfer* the gold. I should like to beautify *old*
Jerusalems. I would pave the streets of bad
Nineveh, of wicked Babylon. I would show Thy
gems to the Gentiles, Thy pearls to the outcast
poor. I should be glad to bring a breath of the
glassy sea into the lanes and alleys of the working
day. Even to *heaven* would I be led "for Thy
name's sake."

THE PECULIARITY OF CHRISTIAN LOVE

"Love envieth not."—1 COR. XIII. 4.

CHRISTIAN love is the only kind of love in which there is no rivalry, no jealousy. There is jealousy among the lovers of art; there is jealousy among the lovers of song; there is jealousy among the lovers of beauty. The glory of *natural* love is its monopoly, its power to say, "It is mine." But the glory of Christian love is its refusal of monopoly. The spiritual artist—the man who paints Christ in his soul—wants no solitary niche in the temple of fame. He would not like to hear any one say, "He is the first of his profession; there is not one that can hold the candle to him." He would be very sad to be distinguished in his profession of Christ, marked out as a solitary figure. The gladdest moment to him will always be the moment when the cry is heard, "Thy brother is coming up the ladder also; thy brother will share the inheritance with thee."

O Thou who art the dear love of my heart, I

monopolisation of heart

would not have Thee love me alone. I would not desire to monopolise Thy heart. I would not claim Thee as my solitary possession. I would have Thee to love me always, to love me everywhere, to love me perfectly—but not to love me only. It is not merely that I am not jealous of my brother; I am very jealous for *Thee*. If I alone possessed Thee it would narrow Thee, limit Thee, circumscribe Thee. My Christ, I would not have Thee narrowed—not for all the pride of being the centre of Thy universe. I would not have Thee lowered to gratify my pride. If I am better than other men, I dare not, with the publican, thank Thee for that. Rather would I pray against my own distinctiveness. I would beat upon my breast and say : " Break the solitude, O Lord ! Deprive me of this monopoly of goodness ! Destroy my pre-eminence in Thy sight ! Remove my isolated splendour on the mountain-top with Thee ! Bring up the crowd at the foot of the hill to share my glory—to love and be loved like me ! Let us sing one song ; let us wear one wreath ; let us tell one tale ; let us feel one joy ; let us fill one house ; let us tread one court ; let us speak one tongue ; let us offer one heart of praise ! Feed Thy sheep, lest I love Thee more than they ! "

THE SABBATH OF THE HEART

" And God blessed the seventh day, and sanctified it : because that in it He had rested from all His work."—GEN. II. 3.

CREATION goes from the wing to the nest. It begins with the Spirit moving, and it ends with the Spirit resting. But observe, it is the rest of a *spirit*. What is the rest of a spirit ? It is the opposite of a body's rest. The body rests when it has reached exhaustion ; the spirit, when it has reached satisfaction. The body reposes when it has closed its eyes on everything ; the spirit reposes when it has opened its eyes on its own image. God could not rest until He beheld His likeness in the pool. Without that likeness the pool was stagnant, and stagnancy is not the spirit's rest. My heart can never find repose until it has found something like itself, something made in its own image. Then alone it meets with that delicious thing, reciprocity. Reciprocity is the Sabbath of the heart. It is a Sabbath bell ringing across the snow. It tells me there is somewhere in the void a house of kindred

26

The Sabbath of the Heart

sympathy where I can find communion, fellowship, response. When I want to rest in my body, I wish no one to speak to me. But when I want to rest in my spirit, I wish to be spoken to. It is a *voice* I crave for—the answer of a heart to my heart, the throb of a soul to my soul, the reply of a life to my life. My spirit will rest when it finds its other self.

O Thou Divine Man, I shall find it in Thee. Thou art that for which I have been waiting, without which I have been weak. It is my want of rest that has made my want of service; my spirit in its Gethsemane has been sleeping for sorrow. Thou comest to awake me out of sleep, to wake me by Thy rest. When I repose in Thee, I shall repose in nothing else. The calm of my heart shall give it wings. There is no flight so high as that of the bird that has been in Thy bosom. Rest my heart, O Lord, that it may soar! It has no pinions out of Thy sunshine. It sings in Thy beams; it plays in Thy smile; it flutters in Thy nest; it flies in Thy pavilion; it leaps to Thy music; it stirs to Thy peace; it gathers endless strength when it makes an end in Thee. If I sleep in Thee, I shall do well.

THE SAFEGUARDING OF FIRST IMAGININGS

"God saw that every imagination of the thoughts of man's heart was only evil continually."—GEN. VI. 5.

THIS is a very spiritual perception to find place in so old a book. One would have thought that so antique a document would have taken a more outward view of the situation. We should have expected it to say, " The Lord saw that man was perpetrating deeds of appalling atrocity." Instead of that it is not the deed at all it emphasises; it is the imaginings. And this old document is right. It is before its time. In an age when men looked only at the act, the writer of Genesis fixed his eye on the imagination. The imagination was to him what *God* saw—the main part of the process. You and I, in all cases of moral corruption, should follow the example of this ancient seer; we should seek the cause, not in the deed of to-day, but in the ideal of yesterday. All corruption begins with an evil imagination, in other words, with the admiration of a bad ideal. The origin of sin is a

28

false model of greatness. A boy becomes selfish because he is taught that great people are those who possess much. He becomes violent, because he has nursed the thought that true heroism is fighting heroism. He becomes irreligious because he has been told that independence is manliness. The picture-book is the child's first educator; and it educates either for good or ill. It educates for ill when pictures of badness are beautifully painted. That becomes an imagination of the *heart*. Evil is made attractive, fair, heroic—an object to be sought for, a thing to be desired.

Ye who train the young—parents and teachers —beware of the first gallery in which you put the child! Beware of the earliest pictures which its heart will hold! They are the germ-cells of the spirit—they will make or mar. Beware how you suffer a bright colour to light upon a vicious form! The vice will grow dim to the eye, but the bright colour will remain. There is only one picture that the child's heart can safely hold; it is the form of Jesus. Put it there early—before all things! Let it be the first painting in the soul—the child's first ideal of greatness! Let the morning message of heroism be a message of unselfishness! Not on Cæsar, not on Alexander, not on Napoleon, let the opening eye be centred; point it to Jesus! Let it

Earliest pictures are germ-cells of spirit which will make or mar

gaze on the glory of what man calls weak, unfit for survival! Let it see the strength of gentleness, the courage of meekness, the might of restraint, the victory of forgiveness, the majesty of patience, the triumph of peacemaking, the manliness of compassion, the Divineness of sacrifice! Let it behold the splendour of that epitaph, " Himself He cannot save," the lustre of that inscription, " Obedient unto death "! Let it mark the heroism of that bloodiest of battlefields where Love stood dauntless to receive its mortal wound! Let it catch the light of the Dolorous Way, the sheen of Gethsemane, the glow of Calvary—till the heart of the child shall cry, " When I grow up, I will be a Christ!" Then will the tempter vanish, then will the kingdom come; for the victory is already complete when we have imaged the beauty of holiness.

Learn to image the beauty of Holiness

THE SOURCE OF UNREST

" I came not to send peace, but a sword."—MATT. x. 34.

THE advent of new light is always the breaking of old peace. We often speak of getting tired of things. When that happens you may be sure it is because a new thing has come. It is not fickleness that makes a child weary of its toy; it is the sight of something higher. All unrest is born of clearer vision. I have no doubt that, to St. John, Patmos was quite tolerable till he saw the New Jerusalem. When he looked upon a sea of glass he began to wish that there was no more sea of water; but before that time he was probably quite satisfied with the water. How small and narrow looked the streets of your own town when you came back from the great metropolis! Previous to your going they seemed splendid, ample, roomy; but one minute of London put them in the shade. So is it with the city of Christ; it spoils me for everything. The moment I rest my eye on it, I can rest it on nothing else. It turns my palaces into hovels; it makes my mountains low. The things which used to be gain to me I count loss in the presence of an all-excelling glory. I may even be more easily fretted than of yore; but for the love of God, I should. A man's unrest is in proportion to his standard. He who knows nothing of the calm depths of God may be content with the tossing of the wave; but the man who has gazed on the glassy sea will wish no other sea, will long for the time when storm shall be no more.

This, O Son of Man, is the cross Thou bringest me. I cannot escape that cross. I cannot look on Thee without being disenchanted with the world. Before Thy coming I was at peace. Everything was to me perfect; I said, "It is good to be here; let me build my tabernacle here." But, at Thy coming, the cloud fell. Everything of mine went into hopeless shadow. My large rooms looked meagre; my gold became dim; my songs ceased to inspire me; my books had a want in them; my entertainments left me thirsty; my ambitions most disappointed where they were most fulfilled. Would I rather be without my cross? Not I. Do I deem that the former days were better than these? Yes; as a beast counts betterness. They had no shadow because they had no light. Thou hast brought the shadow because Thou hast brought the light. Thou hast revealed mortality through immortality. Thou hast shown me night through day. Thou hast taught me silence by music. Thou hast instructed me in the thorn by the bloom of the rose. Thou hast made me know deformity by the sight of Thy beauty. Thou hast told me by Thy life what it is to be dead. Thou hast given me a vision of earth through the gates of heaven. It is the brightness of Thy coming that has consumed my paltry fires; my sword has entered by Thy peace.

Sword and peace

THE ORGAN OF DIVINE KNOWLEDGE

"Eye hath not seen, nor ear heard, the things which God hath prepared for them that love Him. But God hath revealed them unto us by His Spirit."—I COR. II. 9, 10.

EVERYTHING is seen by its own glass; everything looks foolish when seen through any other glass. Music is meaningless when addressed only to the eye; painting has no message to the ear. The deep things of man can only be seen by their own faculty. So is it with the deep things of God. There are things in religion which are mysteries to every organ but one—the spirit of love. There are depths which love alone can fathom. I hear of Divine suffering; I look through the glass of reason and pronounce it a mystery. I say, Could an Infinite Being be limited by human trials! But the moment I learn what love is I see through another glass. I see that, the more infinite love is, the more limited must its possessor be. I see that if God be love He not only can, but must, suffer more than others. I see that if He were less infinite He would be less limited, less crushed

34

by the sorrows around Him. It is the fulness of His love that makes Him so susceptible to pain—the pain of others; it is His majesty that crucifies Him; His cross is made from His crown.

O Thou whose name is Love, by Thine own spirit Thy mysteries are manifest to me. I understand Thy cross the moment I understand Thy glory. If Thy glory were the kingdom and the power, I should think Thy cross what the Romans thought it—foolishness. But Thy glory is love, and therefore Thy fetter is Thy wing. Thy burdens are the gems of Thy crown. I understand why it is that all the sorrow came to Thee, and not to me; it was because Thou wert so infinitely more loving. I understand why the penalty of sin fell on Thy bosom, not on mine. Mine had not love enough to bear that pain. It would have been a mystery if it had fallen on aught but Thee. It was the Divine in Thee, not the human, that made Thee suffer. We speak of Thy humiliation. Thy humiliation was not Thy cross; it was that which hindered Thy cross. Thy cross exalted Thee; every nail was a badge of royalty, every thorn a wreath of majesty. Thy cross *became* Thee, O Christ; it was the fitting raiment of the king. It became Thee better than the crown I meant for Thee—the hosannas to the son of David. God forbid that I should see Thy glory in aught beside! It is all limpid-clear when seen through the glass of love.

THE SOLEMNITY OF YOUTH

"Put off thy shoes from off thy feet, for the place whereon thou standest is holy ground."—EXOD. III. 5.

THESE words were first uttered to a nation's youth. They are strange words to be addressed to youth of any sort. They are an exhortation to a feeling of solemnity. We do not commonly think of youth as a solemn time. We expect it to be an ardent time, an enthusiastic time, a hopeful time; but the last thing we should associate with it is solemnity. And yet I think we are wrong. I believe youth to be the most solemn of all seasons—more solemn than the hour of death. There is an analogy between youth and death. Both are beginnings, enterings upon the unknown; but they are beginnings of a very different kind. In death I am passive; I am in the hands of One, and that One the highest. But in youth I am in the hands of three; I am between three currents —my brother, myself and God. And they are cross-currents; they are impelling different ways. Mine moves inward; my brother's moves outward;

37

God's moves upward. Death is not a battle-field ; I am a captive there ; God is all in all. But youth is a battle-field ; God, my brother, and I, are on conflicting sides, and there is likely to be strife. No wonder I am solemn before the burning bush of the morning !

O thou, who standest before that glowing fire, put off thy shoes from off thy feet ! My cry to thee beyond all things is, " Be solemn ! " Many will tell thee to be aspiring ; " the aspirations of youth " has become a proverbial phrase. And yet I think aspiration should be thy *second* thought. I would have thy first thought one of reverent fear. Many will bid thee mount up with eagle's wings. I would have thee to feel at first a paralysis of the wings. The morning sun is beating upon thee and beckoning thee upward ; God calls to thee out of the fire. But there are obstructions to thy flight ; there are frictions of the air which impede thy soaring. There are winds of passion which would divert thee from thy sun. There are gusts of pride that would drive thee from thy goal. There are storms of temptation which fain would clog thy climbing. Life is more dangerous than death ; thy wayward heart misguides thee ; thy brother's hand misleads thee. It is less fearful to be alone with thy God than to dwell in thy God's disputed presence. When thou standest by the beautiful gate of life's temple, it is thy time to pray. Be it thine, like the angels, to veil thy face with thy wings ere thou fliest! Be it thine to hide thyself in the secret of God's pavilion ere thou soarest into the sky! Remember thy Creator in the days of thy youth, for the place of the burning bush is arduous ground.

THE COMFORT OF GOD'S PARDON

"Speak ye comfortably to Jerusalem, and cry unto her, that her iniquity is pardoned; for she hath received of the Lord's hand double for all her sins."—ISA. XL. 2.

How strange a sound of comfort! Is there not something grotesque about it? To be told that I am pardoned is doubtless consolatory; but to be told that I am pardoned because I have got double punishment is surely fitted to irritate rather than to please. Nay, but it is not the *punishment* God speaks of; it is the reparation. Is there any pure soul that would like to be pardoned without atonement, without paying back even more than he took away! If I have done my brother a wrong and there comes to me a voice through the silent air, "Be of good cheer, it will be all forgiven," would that really give me cheer? Not if mine were a pure soul. I would ask something more than my pardon—the reparation of my wrong. I would ask to pay, to pay more. I would ask not only to be allowed to restore, but to be allowed to enrich—not simply to fill the coffers I have

40

emptied, but to place a larger treasure in their room. There is no sweetness in my pardon until I am told that my deed has been washed away. — From Thy hands alone, O Lord, can I receive a pardon that shall comfort, because from Thy hands alone can they whom I have injured be recompensed. Men speak of Thy forgiving love in redeeming from the fires of hell, but there is no fire so hot to me as the remorse for yesterday. I have injured my brothers a hundred times. Some of them are beyond the reach of my remedy. Who shall make it up to them when they have passed out of my hands! If it cannot be made up to them, it will not be made up to me. Pity will not do it; mercy will not do it; pardon will not do it; love will not do it; heaven itself will not do it. If I have caused eternal pain, I think I would rather have pain than joy. How could I sit beside Lazarus if I knew that I had helped Dives to his seat below! Thou alone canst satisfy me, O Lord. Only from Thy hands can I receive the reparation of my sin. Many of my victims have passed beyond me; but they have not passed beyond Thee. Thou holdest all things in the hollow of Thy hand. Make it up to them, my God! Pay them what I owe! Recompense their loss! Compensate their tears! Mitigate the pain which I have brought them! Nay, better, turn the pain into a glory! If I have sent Jacob to lie on a pillow of stone, make it to him a place for angels! If I have driven Joseph into a dungeon, lead him through it to a throne! If I have cast Moses on the rude waters, bear him on their bosom to a happy shore! If I have helped to wound the Son of Man, make His cross the world's crown! My pardon shall be perfect comfort when Thou hast redeemed my sin.

THE FEAST BEFORE SUFFERING

" With desire I have desired to eat this passover with you before I suffer."—LUKE XXII. 15.

WHY had our Lord this desire? One would think the suffering so serious a thing as to make the passover a matter of no account. Nay; it was just because the suffering was so serious that the passover *was* of account. For what is the idea of the passage? It is that joy is the best preparation for sorrow. Strange as we may think it, it is not pain that helps us to bear pain; it is the remains of gladness. Take any moment of your grief, and ask what it is that has kept you from breaking down utterly. You will find it is some comfort in reserve. We are saved by the patch of blue sky. Particularly are we saved by the patch of blue sky in the firmament of love. It is easier to bear a thing when I am surrounded by those whom I love. I think I could endure consciously a physical operation if one whom I loved were to hold my hand. So felt the Son of Man. He wanted to arm Himself with sunbeams before He suffered. He

43

desired to warm Himself at the fire of the human heart before He went out into the night cold. He felt that the flood would be easier to breast if He first saw the rainbow ; He sought to be transfigured by the light of joy ere He was called to enter into the cloud.

O Thou who still art suffering on the cross of human sin, let me strengthen Thee by my love ! It is a bold prayer. We often ask Thy strength for conflict, but Thou hast taught us that we can strengthen *Thee*. Thou art going forth as of yore up the Dolorous Way; take the passover with me before Thou goest ! Come into my pavilion and warm Thyself at the fire ! for it is toward evening and the day is far spent. I would anoint Thee for Thy burial, O Christ. I would bring Thee the alabaster box in advance of the pain. I feel that the alabaster box will mitigate the pain. There are angels that strengthen us before we suffer ; let me be such to Thee! Let me tell Thee of my love, my deathless love ! Let me speak to Thee of my faith, my cloudless faith ! Let me sing to Thee of my hope, my immortal hope! Let me offer Thee on the road to Jerusalem the sight of a fig-tree where the fruit is already come ! So shalt Thou eat the passover before Thy suffering, and my hand shall be privileged to pluck a thorn from Thy brow.

THE EXALTATION OF HUMILITY

"He that shall humble himself shall be exalted."—
MATT. XXIII. 12.

I DO not understand the words to mean that if
we begin by having a low opinion of ourselves,
God will ultimately give us a high one. If humility
is not to be a permanent virtue it is hard to see
why it should exist at all. But I take the words
to mean that if a man becomes perfectly humble
his humility itself will become his greatness. Have
you ever felt what a compliment it is, when a man
is possessed of any special virtue, to be able to say
of him, "It is no merit; he cannot help it!" To
my mind, it is the climax of all compliment. In
the world of *intellect* every man would deem it so.
What do we mean by the word "genius"? Is it
not simply that a man cannot *help* being great?
He sings or paints, not because he can, but
because he must, because there is within him a
breath of inspiration which will not let him go
until he has blessed the world. That is genius—
the thing which all men reverence. They reverence

the man because he cannot help it, because he is dominated by a power higher than his own. His greatness is his prostration; his glory is his dependence; his crown is the fact of being conquered; he is exalted by humility.

O Thou Divine Love, Thou art the genius of the *heart*. The moment Thou comest, I say, " I cannot help it." Before Thou comest, I have power to do good or to do bad as I like. But when Thou enterest, my own will dies; it becomes Thine. And I feel that when this happens I am not poorer but richer, that I have not lost but gained. I never really prevail until my own power is lamed in the fight; I never conquer till I can fight no more. Come and conquer me, Thou overmastering Love! It is the wrestling of my will against Thee that makes me small. My independence of Thee is my night; I shall cease to wrestle when the day breaks. I must wrestle when I have only duty and conscience; and when I win I am proud of myself, for I feel how difficult it has been. But when Thou comest, O Love, there will be no difficulty. I shall no longer have strength to strive. I shall lie passive upon Thy bosom; I shall lean helpless on Thine arm; I shall be borne resistless in Thy chariot. My pride shall be that I have no will; my soul shall make its boast in the Lord; my charm shall be my chain; my peace shall be my prison; my faith shall be my fetters; my beauty shall be my binding; my courage shall be my constraint; my strength shall be my subduing; my grace shall be Thy grasp upon my hand. Truly I am only exalted in the deepest vale.

GOD'S PROMISE OF HAPPINESS

"Thou shalt make them drink of the river of Thy pleasures."
—Ps. xxxvi. 8.

GOD never keeps the best wine to Himself; He makes His people drink from the river of His own pleasures. It is a marvellous thought that a finite creature should be allowed to have infinite joy. What is infinite joy? It is not so much joy beyond bounds as joy beyond boundaries. It is the joy in everything that is outside of myself. The river of God's pleasures is the happiness in others being happy. Its peculiarity is told in the book of Genesis; it *went out* of Eden, and from thence it was parted, and became four heads. That is ever its description. It will not remain in its own Eden. It goes out from its personal joy. It breaks its own unity. It insists on dividing itself, sharing itself. Often have I thought of these words: "When Thou shalt make His soul an offering for sin, the pleasure of the Lord shall prosper in His hands." One would think there was no prosperity about it. Was it not a

48

sacrifice ? Yes ; but the pleasure of the Lord *is* sacrifice. It is the joy of giving joy, and therefore of giving up. It is the gladness of parting with a portion of the waters. It is the making of the wine of Cana by shedding the blood of Calvary.

My soul, do not say to thyself, "What is the good of being a Christian ? " It is true those who are not have joy as well. But thy Lord never promised thee a monopoly of joy ; He promised thee a monopoly of the river of His pleasures. It is not thy happiness that marks thee out ; it is the *kind* of thy happiness. There are joys which belong to the world. They are not bad ; yet one need not be a saint to have them. But this is a joy which saints alone can share. It is unique, it is peculiar, it is the stamp of Heaven. There are many ways of being blest ; but it is a great thing to be the "blessed of the *Father*"—to hear the words, " I was hungry and ye gave Me meat ; I was thirsty and ye gave Me drink ; I was a stranger and ye took Me in." Enter thou into the joy of thy Lord ! Enter into the gladness of making glad ! Enter into the rest of giving rest ! Enter into the peace of shedding peace ! Launch thy boat on the river that makes glad God's city ! Let the winter's ice of thy

heart be melted, even though it be by fire, that thou mayst embark in that ship wherein thy Lord saileth! The river of God's pleasure flows into the ocean of His love.

THE CROSS NO LOSS

"I am not come to destroy, but to fulfil."—MATT. v. 17.

CHRIST is the only physician of the soul who does not restore by destroying; all other helpers cure by lopping off a limb. It is possible to cure in such a way. It is possible to make me good by deadening me. You can stop my flight into danger by depriving me of my wing. Many a child has been made obedient by destroying its power of will. Many a youth has been made moral by the mere exhaustion of his passions. Many a man has come to long for Heaven, only because he has lost the chance of ambition on earth. You may vanquish temptation at too dear a price—you may become too cold to feel. The benumbed heart will do no wrong. It will neither strive nor cry, neither plot nor scheme, neither fret nor scold; yet it is not thereby justified. It strives not, because it cares not; it has no temptation, because it has no desire. It has ceased to hate, because it has ceased to love. It is salvation by death.

Not so is *Thy* coming, O Thou Saviour of Men. Thou dost not make the perfume by trampling on the flower. Man often gets the fragrance of a harmless life by breaking the ointment box. Not so dost *Thou* call forth life's fragrance. Not by less, but by more love, dost Thou save us; not by diminished life, but by life " more abundant," dost Thou make us beautiful. They tell me that Thou requirest the sacrifice of self. Nay, my Lord, not its sacrifice, but its enlargement. Thou breakest a wall in my room, but it is that I may include my brother's room in mine. Not to destroy, but to fulfil, has the breakage come. I have been living in too small a house; I have been failing to see that my brother is a part of myself; I have been cherishing the delusion that the wall in my room is the limit of my interest. Therefore, Thou hast broken my wall, and let in the light beyond. Thou hast broken my wall and made me say, " I and my brother are one "; Thou hast broken my wall, and hast widened the range of my self-love. I have not sacrificed myself; I have grown into a bigger self. I have not lost respect for the members of my body, but I have added to their number the members of Thine. I have not ceased to care for the calamities of life, but I have learned to say of these calamities, "Inasmuch as they did it unto the least, they have done it unto me." My soul has not been *crucified* by yielding to Thy cross; Thou art not come to destroy, but to fulfil.

THE UTILITY OF BEAUTY

" To what purpose is this waste."—MATT. XXVI. 8.

THIS is the earliest protest against external beauty in the service of Christ. Mary was serving Christ's own person—pouring on His head a rich and costly perfume. The disciples objected to the act on the ground that it was merely ornamental, not useful. They said that a box of ointment, however precious, had nothing to do with their salvation. Were they not preparing for eternity, and was not this a perishable riches! Were they not told to seek the *un*seen, and was not this a thing to please the eye! Were they not taught that Jesus was to be served by *spiritual* things, and was not this a trinket of the hour, which would not *last* an hour! So thought the earliest Philistines in the camp of Jesus. But they made one great mistake —and it has been repeated by their successors. They thought that a thing could be beautiful without being useful. It cannot. To me the main value of beauty is its usefulness. I regard a scene of beauty as exercising a *mechanical* power—

54

as mechanical as the steam-engine, and more effective. The steam-engine can move heavy bodies; but a thing of beauty can move heavy hearts. Very unaccountable is this moving power of beauty; it often acts without an ally. I feel disconsolate, pessimistic, despairing; I weigh everything and find it wanting. Suddenly there streams a sunbeam from the hill and there is wafted a breath from the sea, and in a moment all is changed. My clouds vanish; my pessimism melts; my gloom dies away. Nothing has happened to *make* it glide away—nothing but the streaming of the sunbeam and the wafting of ocean's breath. But these are, for the day and hour, my Father's sacraments to me. They are very fugitive things—more fugitive than was the ointment from the box outpoured. That special sunbeam was superseded by another ray. That special breath of ocean fainted on the bosom of the hour. But they had lifted my soul to a city on the hill, and when they were gone my soul still rested there. Who would measure their use by their duration! One special strain of music may keep me all night in joy.

My soul, despise not the power of beauty! The sunbeam and the song are sacraments of thy *Father*. They are the bread broken outside the

55

Dissipation of gloom

Moving heavy hearts.

church—the bread broken to the multitude. We have our sacraments with *Christ;* but there are times of desert life when we need our *Father's* bread. Uncover thy head before the sacrament of beauty! Bow reverently at the distribution of Nature's sacred elements! Survey the passion of Divine love that meets thee in the shed blood of the sunbeam! Behold the outpouring of the cup that blesses thee in the dew and the rain! Adore the universal communion that makes its light to rise on the evil and the good! Forget not at morn or evening to keep thy Father's feast; for the wafting of ocean's breath is the wafting of the Father's incense, and the breaking of the sunbeam is the breaking of the Father's bread.

THE MINISTRY OF JOY TO GRIEF

"There shall be no night there."—REV. XXI. 25.

How, then, can there be a serving of the sorrowful? You tell me that heaven is a land of ministration. How can it be so if my heart is to have the joy of morning? Can joy minister to grief? Yes, joy alone *can*. It is not night that ministers to night; it is nightlessness. To meet the clouds of others I should myself be clear. If I have lost a child and my neighbour across the street has lost a child, the common experience does not itself make either of us helpful to the other. To be helpful to my neighbour it is not enough that I have passed into the same valley; I must have passed *through*. " Yea, though I walk through the valley" is a saying of deep significance. It is not the *darkness* that makes me a comforter; it is seeing the exit at the foot of the lane. It is being able to say, "*I* have passed through; you will also."

O Thou who art training me to be a ministering spirit, let me enter into Thy joy! Ere I go with

57

Thoughts for Life's Journey

Thee into the wilderness, let me stand with Thee by the glad streams of Jordan; let me see the opened heavens and the descending dove! It was by the joy set before Thee that Thou didst bear my cross; how else shall I bear *Thine!* Thou hast said that Thy yoke of ministration is easy and its burden light; but to whom? To those who have found rest to their souls. Thou hast bidden me learn of *Thee;* and that is *Thy* experience. It was the gleam of Olivet that made possible Thy Calvary. In vain shall I seek my brother's night if there is night in my own soul. In vain shall I stand by when he drinks the cup of sorrow, in vain shall I *participate* in his cup of sorrow, if I have not seen the sparkle in the bitter draught. Show me that sparkle, O Lord! Reveal to me the sunlight in the cup! I would not go forth to help the sad on the mere ground that I have myself been sad. I would see Thy crown in my own waters before I say to my brother, "Peace, be still." Reveal to me Thy gold ere I go! Let me stand with Thee one hour on the mountain ere I descend to meet the valley! Let me catch the morning rays ere I confront the evening shadows! My heart will be a minister to the night when there is no night there.

THE CITY OF GOD

"New Jerusalem, which cometh down out of heaven."—
Rev. iii. 12.

ALL the *old* Jerusalems go *up*. The cities of
this world are ambitious to beautify themselves.
They have the pride of the Tower of Babel. So
eager are they to ascend that the upper part of
them leaves the lower behind, and there is a great
gulf fixed between rich and poor. The Jerusalems
of earth are ever flying from their lowly places—
sending their best men into the heights where they
shall escape the cry of the vulgar crowd. But it
is not so with the New Jerusalem, the city of my
God. This has ever a descending attitude. Its
goal is toward the places from which the cities of
the world wish to fly; it moves downward. It is
afraid to reap a solitary privilege, a privilege not
shared by all. It knows well that its *high* places
must catch the sun; but it wants its vales to catch
it too. It is anxious for the masses—those that
toil and spin, those that hunger and thirst, those
that work and weep. It would bring the grapes

of Eshcol to the lips that are parched, the rose of Sharon to the eyes that are weary, the chariots of Israel to the feet that are lame. It would take foundling children to the arms of shelter. It would bring the leper from the tombs. It would lead blind Bartimæus from the cold streets. It would make a place for the beggar Lazarus *within* the gates. It would let Christ speak to the demoniac. It would give penitent Peter a new commission after his great denial. It would light a warm fire for Magdalene when she has washed the Divine feet with her tears.

Thou art descending, O city of God; I see thee coming nearer and nearer. Tongues are dead, prophecies are dying; but charity is born. Our castles rise into the air and vanish; but love is bending lower every day. Man says, "Let us make a tower on earth which shall reach unto heaven"; but God says, "Let us make a tower in heaven which shall reach unto earth." O descending city, O humanitarian city, O city for the outcast and forlorn, we hail thee, we greet thee, we meet thee! All the isles wait for thee—the lives riven from the mainland—the isolated, shunted, stranded lives! They sing a new song at thy coming, and the burden of its music is this, "He hath prepared for *me* a city"!

THE FAULT OF OUR FIRST ASPIRINGS

" Let us build a tower, whose top may reach unto heaven."—
Gen. XI. 4.

When man uttered these words, he was a child.
Children are very ambitious—more ambitious than
grown-up people.   Grown-up people ask things
that are possible ; children cry for the supernatural.
I think our sense of power increases in proportion
as we are undeveloped.   One would imagine that
a little child, coming within the gates of this
universe, would have a startled feeling, and that
the startled feeling would gradually wear off as he
advanced on life's journey.   In truth, it is all the
reverse ; we get startled *as we go*.   Our first view
of the golden gates is not appalling ; it frightens
neither the child nor the savage.   I do not think
wonder belongs to the earliest mind either of race
or individual. To both alike the sky can be scaled ;
the motto of each is this, " Let us make a tower,
whose top may reach unto heaven ! "   This world
is a place where human beings are taught to climb ;

but it is to climb down. It is quite natural for us to go *up*. The writer of the Book of Job says, " Man is born to trouble, as the sparks fly upward." I think he must have meant, "Man is born to fly upward like the sparks, and therefore he is troubled." At all events, that is true. Our early dangers come from our early daringness—not from our early feebleness. Young Adam always begins with the biggest tree and always gets a fall. God's education of the earth is a series of lessons in " how to descend "—in the moderation of desire. Christian prayer itself is a moderation of desire. It is a refusal any longer to say of everything, " It is mine." It is the refusal to ask that which will lift me above other people. It is the cry to have my garments parted among the multitude. It is the impulse, the determination, the instinct, to *share*.

Lord, break my primitive tower! It is built with a child's arrogance—not with a man's humility ; break my primitive tower! My feeblest moments are my most grasping moments—I am never such an egotist as in the cradle ; break my primitive tower! Like the sparks, I have been born to fly upwards, and to leave my brother behind. I need a second birth—a power to fly downward. I need more *weight* on the wings ; every weight will be to me " a weight of glory."

The Fault of Our First Aspirings

The glory of the bird is its boundlessness; but the glory of the man is his boundary. Limit my desires, O Lord! Restrain the flight of my personal prayers! Put a weight on the wings of each individual wish—the remembrance of my brother! In my childhood I cried for all things; in manhood I dare not. I can still pray without ceasing, but I can no longer pray without limit. What if I ask the gold that was meant for another! What if I seek the place that was made for another! What if I claim the work that was planned for another! Methinks the pauses of prayer are more noble than its flights. In these pauses I say, "Not my will, but Thine." Are they not to Thee the finest parts of the music, O my Father! There is no architecture so beautiful to Thee as my arrested tower—my tower arrested that another may have room. Never let me build, even in my prayers, a house with so many mansions for myself that I cannot say to my brother, "I have prepared a place for *you*"!

THE THREE CHORDS OF LOVE

" Thou shalt love the Lord thy God with all thy heart, and with all thy soul, and with all thy mind."—MATT. XXII. 37.

THERE are three kinds of love—perhaps rather I should say, three instruments on which love plays. It may manifest itself through the heart, through the soul, or through the mind. My love for you may be either practical, admiring, or communing. The love of the heart is practical; it ministers in common things. The love of the soul is admiration; it looks upon a far-off glory and longs to be near it. The love of the mind is communion; it has touched a point of equality with its object; it can listen and respond. A mother's love for her child is that of the heart; it is helpful. A poet's love for Nature is that of the soul; it is wondering, admiring. A friend's love for a friend is that of the mind; it is intellectual sympathy—communion. I think our love for God plays successively each of these tunes. We begin with the heart; we say, " Our Father "; we try to *work* for our Father. By-and-by the vision of *wonder*

64

breaks upon us—the love of the soul; we bow with admiration before the mysteries of the universe. At last comes the glad morning—the love of the mind; we begin to *know* God—to commune with Him, to speak with Him face to face as a man speaketh with his friend. That is the *manhood* of our love.

My God, I long to reach this third stage—this summer of my pilgrimage. I have seen Thee as a child sees its father; it was a sweet feeling, yet it was a feeling of dependence—it did not bring me quite *near* Thee. I have seen Thee again as the poet sees his promised land of beauty; it was a grand vision, yet it was a vision which dwarfed the passing day, which overshadowed the common hour. I want more than that. I want to feel Thee by my side, to walk with Thee, to talk with Thee. I may love with the heart where I have no communion of mind; I may love with the soul where I have imperfect communion of mind; but to love with the mind is to understand. Not my sense of dependence is Thy deepest joy; not my gaze of wonder is Thy brightest sunshine. The love that lights Thee most is the love that can *understand* Thee—the love of the mind. I would be called no more servant, but friend. Hitherto I have been content to receive Thy *protection*; but that will not break Thy solitude. If I am always to be a child, there will be no companionship for Thee. Shalt Thou tread the winepress alone— with none to understand Thee! Shall Thy Gethsemane hour have only my pity, only my wonder! I have seen a child weep for its father's pain without knowing why its father grieved; it was the love of the heart, but not yet the love of the mind. Not so would I come into Thy Garden, O God. I would come to comprehend Thee, to know Thee, to appreciate Thee. I would *forget* my dependence. I would rise into Thy fellowship, Thy communion. I would cease to follow; I would walk side by side. I would share Thy burden; I would adopt Thy name; I would assimilate Thine accent; I would appropriate Thy cause. Give me this final love, this mental love, O Lord; for he that loves Thee with the mind loves Thee also with the heart and with the soul.

COMFORT IN PROSTRATION

"Thou compassest my lying down."—Ps. cxxxix. 3.

OUR moments of "lying down" are not generally deemed Divine moments. We can understand the previous words, "Thou compassest my *path*,"— my *walk* of life. That is a sphere of action— where it is possible for us to do great things. But that our times of quiescence should be times of Divine interest, that our seasons of inaction should be seasons of the presence of God—this is strange indeed! Yes, and it is as comforting as it is strange. You and I are often called to experience these moments of "lying down." There are times when, in the language of another psalm, our strength is "weakened in the way." There are seasons when we have to leave the path and go home—go into retirement, into solitude, into seeming uselessness. And the hardest part of these moments is just the sense of having missed our destiny. We have been shunted from the path, we have been made to lie down; and it seems to us as if God had no further place for us beneath the circle of the sun. What a comfort at such moments are these words of the ancient psalmist, "Thou compassest my lying down"! They tell us that the quiescent hour may be a Divine hour, that the seemingly useless moment may be full of God. They tell us that the greatest day of our life may be the day after we have *quitted* the path—the day of our prostration, our pain, our weariness. They tell us that the places where we are forced to lie down may be God's green pastures, that the coming to quiet waters may be God's own leading. The hour which our soul is rejecting may be the hour when the kingdom has come.

O Christ of Calvary, in my days of valley and shadow help me to feel that "Thou art with me"! It is not enough for me to feel that, one day, there will be mountain and sunshine. No; that is only to say Thou wilt be with me in the future. I want Thee now. What I need is not help to leave the valley nor help to clear the shadow. I want to feel that Thou art *in* the valley, that Thou art *in* the shadow. I want my "lying down" itself to be glorified. It is *something* to know that Thou wilt raise me up at the last day—on the day when my discipline is completed; but it is not enough for me. Is the time of my rest to be Godless—without

68

Comfort in Prostration

Thy presence! Is my valley to be a waste place, a useless place, a place where Thou art not! Is my shadow to be an eclipse of *Thee*, a blotting out of Thee! It is not enough to know that to-morrow the cup will pass; I must be able to feel, with Thee, that *to-day* it is "the cup my Father has given me." Reveal to me the glory of Gethsemane! Reveal to me the majesty of my desert hour! Reveal to me the ladder of angels that rose from my couch of clay! Reveal to me the Bethlehem songs that came from my midnight silence! Reveal to me the multitudes in my wilderness— the crowds that waited on me when I thought myself alone! My life will be robbed of half its weariness when I see Thee compassing my "lying down."

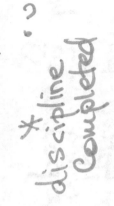

THE CAUSE OF SLOW PROGRESS

"I have loved Thee with an everlasting love; therefore with lovingkindness have I drawn Thee."—JER. XXXI. 3.

I UNDERSTAND the word "drawn" to be used here as the opposite of "driven." I take the meaning to be: "It is because I love you that I do not force you; I desire to *win* by love." We often express surprise that human life does not reveal more traces of God's omnipotence. We see the visible universe subject to inexorable law and yielding submissively to that law. But *man* does not yield submissively; he resists the will of the Eternal. Why should he be allowed to resist? Is he not but an atom in the infinite spaces—these spaces that obey the heavenly mandate? Why not put down his insane rebellion and crush his proud will into conformity with the universal chorus? The Bible gives its answer. It is because love is incompatible with the exercise of omnipotence. Inexorable law can rule the stars; but the stars are not an object of love. Man is an object of love, and therefore he can only be ruled

70

by love—as the prophet puts it, "drawn." Nothing is a conquest for love but the power of drawing. Omnipotence can subdue by driving—but that is not a conquest for love; it is rather a sign that love is baffled. Therefore it is that our Father does not *compel* us to come in. He would have us "drawn" by the beauty of holiness; therefore He veils all that would force the will. He hides the glories of Heaven. He conceals the gates of pearl and the streets of gold. He reveals not the river of His pleasures. He curtains from the ear the music of the upper choir. He obscures in the sky the sign of the Son of Man. He forbids the striking of the hours on the clock of Eternity. He treads on a path of velvet lest the sound of His coming footsteps should conquer by fear the heart that ought to be won by love.

O Thou whose name is Love, it is by that name alone I can explain why things move so slow. But in the light of that name I understand; the pauses become musical, the halts are stages of the march. I have heard a man express the wish to be in Thy place for one day; he thought he would reform Thy universe. He would have spoiled it. He would have conquered the refractory child by killing its will. Not thus would Thy Divine Fatherhood be victorious. Thou wouldst rather draw by the cross than drive by the crown. Often it seems to me that this world of Thine appeals more to the heart than to any other part of my nature. It is not all beautiful, it is not all poetical, it is not all intelligible, it is not all practical; but it is every inch pathetic. There is pathos in the starry night; there is pathos in the moaning sea; there is pathos in the monotonous stream; there is pathos in the song of birds; there is pathos in the human tear; there is pathos even in the rolling wheels of daily labour. Thou art leading me by weary paths—paths where I feel my brother's pain, paths where I touch my brother's thorn. Had I been a butterfly Thou wouldst have tempted me by roses and hurried me through the field; but because I am a man Thou hast drawn me by the slow cord—the winning of my heart.

CHRISTIAN MESMERISM

"When I am weak, then am I strong."—2 COR. XII. 10.

WHAT does Paul mean? Does he mean that a man is stronger in proportion to his infirmities? No; the weakness Paul speaks of is not infirmity; it is self-surrender. What he says is that nothing helps a man to bear a burden so much as the captivity of the heart to a separate influence. We see a practical illustration of this in the modern process called hypnotism — now accepted as scientific. The subject of it is deemed a weakling because he gives up his will to another; yet he can often do in his weakness what he could not do in his strength—he generally surpasses his normal self. Paul says, " My greatest strength has come from moments of Divine hypnotism; I have never been so able to bear my burden as when my will has been absolutely enthralled by the beauty of another—that peerless Other—Christ." And who does not feel with Paul that the best cure for a burden is not the conscious struggle with it, but my surrender to something else. It makes a great

73

difference to the length of a journey whether you are walking for your health or walking for converse with *me*. The length of the journey is in the former case a burden; and it is an exact type of all the burdens of life. The burdens of two men may be physically equal; their amount may be the same, their weight the same. Yet the sense of heaviness may be very different. He who lifts in love will lift easily. He will have a power coming from his weakness—from the captivity of his will. His weight will be his wing, his fetter will be his force, his prison will be his power; like the phœnix bird, he will rise from his own ashes; his strength will be perfected in weakness.

Make me *Thy* captive, O Christ, and I shall be free. Bind me with *Thy* chain, and I shall be slave to none beside. There are no moments in which I am so weak as when my love is low. When my heart has no master, my life is mastered by all things. I have heard men ask how much water would be deep enough to drown them. I have found that a pool would be deep enough for me without *Thee*. I have found that any calamity would be overwhelming if I had nothing to think of but itself—but *my*self. It is not the weight of my affliction that kills me; it is its monopoly—its entire possession of my soul. Break that monopoly,

74

The length of the journey and Sense of heaviness

Burdens of life

who masters my heart?

Drowning in Affliction or not?

Christian Mesmerism

O Lord! Withdraw my heart from the sole companionship with its grief! I shall never be emancipated from any sorrow except by a new fetter. I shall never conquer my pain till Thou hast conquered my heart. Bring me Thy golden bonds—love's bonds! Bring me Thy silken cord —the cord of devotion! Bring me Thy sparkling chain—the chain of sympathy! There is no mesmerist like my love. In Thee I can forget my pain. In Thee I can taste the bitter as sweet. In Thee I can see new visions on the old spot. In Thee I can become impervious to cold, to hunger, to weariness. In Thee I can lose my natural fears. In Thee I can speak with tongues—I who was once too timid to speak at all. If only I shall steadfastly gaze into Thy face, if only I shall perfectly give up my will to Thine, I shall be " changed into the same image from glory to glory." Mesmerise my will, O Lord!

THE CHRISTIAN SOLDIER'S SHIELD

"Forasmuch then as Christ hath suffered for us in the flesh, arm yourselves likewise with the same mind."—I PETER IV. I.

THESE words were spoken to a military empire. They were spoken amid a people who had raised themselves by the practice of arms. To such a race the exhortation must have been startling. It promised a new kind of armour, a new species of defence. Such a promise must have made the Roman start and look round. But when he saw the proposed armour he must have laughed. It had neither length, breadth, nor thickness. It could not inflict a single wound upon an enemy. Nay, it was itself a wound. The very putting of it on involved mutilation to the man who wore it. "Forasmuch as Christ hath suffered in the flesh, arm yourselves therefore with the same mind." We can understand a Christian exhorted to the spirit of sacrifice; but is not that an exhortation to *divest* yourself of armour! The novelty of Peter's exhortation does not lie in being told to cultivate the mind of Jesus, but in being told that

76

the mind of Jesus is a source of Roman defence. We all admit sacrifice to be a virtue, but we never think of it as a panoply. We have recognised it as a capacity to yield, but we are not accustomed to view it as a capacity to resist. And yet Peter is right. There is no power that resists danger like the sacrificial power of love. If ever a man learned this by experience it was Peter. Whenever he began to sink it was from internal causes. He went out to meet in the morning a storm from which he recoiled at night. Why? Had the storm increased in violence with the circling hours? No. It was exactly the same as in the morning—no less, no more. But in the interval there was something which had *de*creased—Peter's sacrificial love. He had begun to be self-conscious. He had turned his gaze from Jesus; he had directed his eye to the winds and the sea. Therefore the winds and the sea became too strong for him; he had lost his life-belt.

Put on thine armour, O my soul—the armour of self-sacrifice! Not by self-mutilation canst thou put it on; thy sacrifice must come not from thy grief but from thy joy. There *is* a sacrifice which comes from grief, but it is not an armour. Many have fled from the world through disappointment; yet the world has followed them into their solitude.

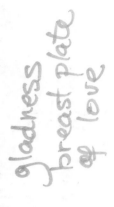

Thoughts for Life's Journey

But *thy* sacrifice must come from gladness, from the greatest joy of the heart—love. Thine armour must be the *breastplate* of love. No selfish thought will protect thee from the sea of temptation. Fear of sickness may defend thee for an hour; dread of public opinion may support thee for a day; but these are swords that soon become blunted. Wouldst thou have an armour against temptation that will keep thee always, everywhere? Get the love of some one pure! Set thy heart upon a high ideal; paint it in the fairest colours; deck it with fancy's loveliest gems! Think of it in the silence; speak to it in the secrecy; dream of it in the night; above all, walk with it in the market-place! Then—call it by what name thou wilt, it will be Christ to *thee*. Thou wilt refuse the flowers of evil; thou wilt reject sin's gilded cup; thou wilt decline pride's glittering bauble. Thine abstinence will come from thine aspiration; thy restraint will flow from the river of thy pleasures; thy sacrifice will be the fruit of thy song. Nothing can crucify the flesh like the joy of the spirit.

THE IMPOTENCE WHICH IS DIVINE

"He saved others ; himself he cannot save."—MATT. XXVII. 42.

THERE is a great difference between inability and incapacity. Incapacity is the absence of a power ; inability may come from the presence of a power. There are two things which may make a man say, " I cannot "—too little life or too much life. Let us say there is a storm at sea. The ship is in the last stage of dilapidation. The life-boats have been lowered and occupied. So full are they that there is only room for one passenger more ; and there are two yet remaining on the vessel. One of these is a paralytic ; like the man at the pool of Bethesda, he has been unfit to push forward ; he cannot save *himself*. The other man has full strength of limb and could take the leap in a moment ; but he has infinite pity for the paralytic ; he feels bound to help him into the boat ; he, too, cannot save himself. Now, what is the difference between these two ? It is not a difference in the degree of helplessness. Both are

79

equally helpless. The contrast lies in the cause of their helplessness. That of the paralytic comes from a sense of weakness; that of the other comes from the sense of a great strength—human love. The one is unfit to save himself by reason of impotence; the other is unfit to save himself by reason of power—power driving him in another direction. The motto of the one is, "The flesh is weak;" the motto of the other is the French saying, "*Noblesse oblige*"—the dignity of my nature makes it impossible for me to do a mean or ignoble thing.

Son of Man, Thou art never so Divine to me as in the hour of Thine impotence. Not on the Mount of wondrous accents, not on the Lake of wondrous deeds, not in the Desert of wondrous charities, art Thou to me so glorious. All spots even of *Thy* journey have paled before the hill of Calvary. Hermon has faded; Tabor has grown dim; Gennesaret's waves have lost their music—but the hill of Calvary keeps green. We worship no hour even of Thine like the hour of Thy disrobing. Whither do the tribes of earth go up? Not to the songs of Bethlehem, not to the voice from heaven, not to the wine of Cana, not to the ruling of the storm, not to Bethsaida's banquet, not to Galilee's gathering, not to Jerusalem's shouts of joy. They come to the hushed hosannas; they come to the withered palm leaves; they come to the broken heart. They bring their anthem to Thy blood, their laurel to Thy grave, their spices to Thy burial. What is it that they *reverence* in Thy setting? Is it feebleness? No, it is power—love's power. It is love that makes Thee passive; it is devotion that makes Thee dumb. Had Thy love been less mighty, Thou couldst have saved Thyself; Thy cross has come from the lustre of Thy crown. Not the lowliness but the love, not the stooping but the strength, not the laying down of life but the Life that laid it down, is the object of our glory. Thou couldst not save Thyself because Thy love was omnipotent.

THE THING GOD WILL NOT LET DIE

"I will write on the tables the words that were in the first tables which thou breakest."—DEUT. x. 2.

How very parsimonious is this promise!—such is the thought which first suggests itself. "I will write on the tables the words that were in the *first* tables"; one is apt to cry, Is that all! The first tables had been broken; it was a lost revelation. We should have thought it would have been replaced, not by a mere repetition, but by something higher. Even if the same song be sung twice by one singer, the second should be better than the first through increased confidence. But why should God be limited to one song! Is not His voice as the sound of many waters! Why should He speak the old things, repeat the old words, reveal the old scenes in the kaleidoscope! Why not press on to a revelation of the future! Why not open the windows of heaven and let us see through! Why keep us in the sphere of prosaic precepts which belong to a child's prayer-book!— "Love God!" "Love man!" "Love parents!"

82

The Thing God will not Let Die

"Love neighbours!" "Love justice, and gentleness, and truth, and purity!" The first tables had the precepts of *earth*; ought not the second tables to have had the precepts of heaven!

My soul, hast thou considered the reason why it is not so? There can be no new morality in heaven; other foundation can no man lay than that which is laid in the first tables. The Ten Commandments are for heaven as much as for earth; death may break these tables, but eternity will reconstruct them. There will never for thee be another moral law; go where thou wilt, thou shalt find the old writing. Many things may be new to thee in the silent land. The eye may have colours unseen to-day. The ear may have sounds unheard to-day. The hand may have measurements undreamed of to-day. There may be new laws of motion; to *think* of a presence may be to *fly* to it. There may be new laws of health; disease may be banished by an act of will. There may be new laws of politics; the faithful servant may be the crowned king. There may be new laws of knowledge; truth may come without training, and science without school. But there will never be new laws of goodness. Wheresoever thou goest, thou shalt never go beyond the writing on the first tables. There will never come to thee a time when righteousness will be other than righteous, purity other than pure, holiness other than holy. The heavens may change, but the heart will abide. Gravity may be suspended, but grace will abide. Lights may be extinguished, but love will abide. Not empty shalt thou enter within the vale; the tables prepared for thee in the wilderness shall meet thee in the house of the Lord. Goodness and mercy shall follow thee, nay, accompany thee—be carried over in thy heart across the flood. Other things may drop from thee in the rush of waters. Vanities will vanish; pride will perish; selfishness will sink; enmities will end. But God has set eternity in thy *heart*, and the things of the heart will cross over. Thy love will leap the flood, thy spirit of sacrifice will bridge the sea. Thy purity shall be transplanted; thy kindness shall be rekindled; thy justice shall be rejuvenated; thy compassion shall be continued; thy tenderness shall be translated; thy charity shall be Elijah's chariot connecting earth with heaven. The writing on thy walls shall appear amid the wreck of Babylon; magnify thine immortality, O my soul!

THE PHYSICAL SYMPATHY OF THE BIBLE

" See how mine eyes have been enlightened because I tasted a little of this honey."—I SAM. XIV. 29.

THESE are the words of Jonathan—one of the best men the world has ever seen. They were spoken at a time of religious revival—one of those seasons when the claims of the soul are apt to be set up in sharp contrast against the claims of the body. The revival in this instance originated with the aristocracy; it came from the palace. In the high places of the land men were proposing to cultivate the soil of the spirit by letting the body starve. They prescribed a life of self-denial for the *sake* of self-denial. They suggested that each should practise outward misery with a view to be inwardly better. To this false idea of sacrifice Jonathan was violently opposed. He showed his opposition in a very wise manner. He did not argue. He did not appeal to books or testimonies. He quoted only one experience—

85

his own, "See how mine eyes have been enlightened, because I tasted a little of this honey."
He says in effect, "I am never so religious as
when my body is well; I never see God so clearly
as when I am physically comfortable." And I
am convinced that Jonathan is right—that in this
matter the general voice of the Jew is right. I do
not think that prosperity is a proof of the favour
of God; but I do think that when a man is
prosperous he is more apt to *favour* God. It is
not purely on secular grounds that we advocate
physical philanthropy. Job says, "In my *flesh*
shall I see God." He speaks truly. He did not
see God when he was in a state of physical
dilapidation; the words might be applied to him,
"In his humiliation his judgment was taken
away." He searched every spot of the universe
to hear a Divine voice that would counteract the
voice of the whirlwind. And yet that voice was
at his very door—in the whirlwind itself. Why
had he to seek for it so long? Simply because
the flesh was weak. The outer man was down.
There was pain in the joints, feebleness in the
nerves, saplessness in the marrow—a general
debility all over. And because the flesh was
defective it failed to convey the message of the
spirit; the telephonic wire was broken, and the

86

listener caught not the voice that was speaking through the gloom.

Lord, I understand now the meaning of that feast where to the famished crowd Thou didst break the bread. I used to think what an opportunity was lost of *teaching* the multitude. It seemed a waste of time to spend in feasting a day which might have been spent in opening the doors of Thy Kingdom. But I see it all now. I see that the hunger was no place for the homily, that the starving flesh could not catch the heavenly flame. I see that the sustenance had to precede the sermon, that the viands had to come before the vision, that the banquet had to be served ere the beatitude was spoken. I bless Thee, Lord, for that humanity to man. Men would have said, "The things of the Spirit come first; convert the people and let them go." But Thy heart saw deeper. It saw that the supper must precede the Sacrament. It refused to send the Life till it had sent the loaves. It would not mock the down-trodden with a tract, the penniless with a prayer, the starving with a psalm; it sought the raising of the body before the salvation of the soul. Son of Man, I marvel at the depth of Thy manhood. *We* have looked upon the multitude and said, "Bring them into the Church"; *Thou* hast looked upon the multitude and cried, " Bring them into the banquet-room." *We* have exclaimed, " Enlighten the eyes of their understanding " ; *Thou* hast said, " Before their eyes see heaven, let their lips taste the honey of earth." Make me partaker of Thy humanity, O Lord !

THE ALTRUISM OF THE HEAVENLY LIFE

" The Lamb shall lead them."—Rev. VII. 17,

We speak of a leading aim in life. In this
world men have various leading aims. Some are
led by ambition, some by pleasure, some by
avarice, some by vanity, some by the thirst for
knowledge. But the Seer of Patmos says that in
the other world the leading aim of life will be
different from any of these; it will be the good of
humanity—what we call altruism. " The Lamb
shall lead them." The lamb is the symbol of
sacrifice. By the leading of the Lamb I understand the Seer to mean the motive power of the
sacrificial spirit. He wishes to convey the idea
that in the future life of the soul every act of man
will be prompted by the desire to help his brother.
You will observe, the difference between heaven
and earth is not the road but the leading—not
the act but the motive. It is not that heaven has
other fountains of water than those which are

89

found on earth ; it is that in heaven we are to be led to those fountains by the Lamb—by the motive of sacrificial love. It makes all the difference in the world whether I am led to a fountain by the spirit of selfishness or by the spirit of sacrifice. *Wealth* is a fountain. Is it pure or impure ? That depends, not on the water, but on what has led me to it. What has been my motive for amassing wealth ? Has it been covetousness, or has it been Christ ? Have I been led by the lust of avarice, or have I been led by the lamb of altruism ? Have I considered only how many sensations it will bring to myself—the rivers of pleasure it will send me, the weight of influence it will lend me, the multitude which, through it, will befriend me ? Or, have I desired it for the good which it can do—for the feeding of the hungry, the clothing of the ragged, the enlightening of the ignorant, the healing of the sick, the beautifying of the temple, the planting of the mission-field, the providing of recreation for the sons of daily toil ? This latter is the "leading of the Lamb." It matters not though the waters be earthly. It counts not though the streams be secular. It lessens not the value, though the gold be from a human mine. If I gather for earth's gladness, if I spend to soothe earth's sadness, if I climb to cleanse earth's badness, I am led to the fountain by the Lamb.

Lamb of God, prepare me for the fashion of *Thy* world! The fashion of our world passeth away. Here, we are led by motives of self-interest—the lust of the flesh and the lust of the eye and the pride of being great. But in Thy world another power shall lead the fashion—Thine own sacrificial life. Prepare me for that world, O Lord! I should not like to be out of fashion in the sweet by-and-by. I should not like to be living for myself when all mankind are living for others. Save me from the loneliness of a solitary aim—an aim that none shall sympathise with! Here, I love my wealth because it enhances me. But they who shall be made rulers over ten cities will only prize their wealth for a brother's joy; the glory of *their* riches will be its power to minister. I should not like to have the ten cities without their glory, to value my own possessions for the old earthly reason. There would be none to share my estimate. Nobody would gratify my thirst for admiration. Nobody would pause and say, " What magnificent fields ! " Nobody would cry, " *There* is a man worth knowing ! " They would all be running after the new fashion—the search for impoverishment—" Enter ye into the

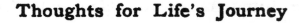

joy of your Lord!" Be that *my* joy, O Christ—
not only then, but now! Be that my joy, O
Christ—the gladness of having something to give!
Be that the radiance of my riches, the prize of my
possessions, the glory of my gold, the shining of
my silver, the fragrance of my fields, the greatness
of my granaries, the majesty of my many
mansions! Then shall I be in the fashion of the
future; I shall be led to my fountains by the
Lamb.

THE BREADTH OF CHRISTIANITY

"An entrance shall be ministered unto you abundantly."—
I PETER I. 2.

WHY an entrance "abundantly"? Are there any degrees between getting in and being shut out? Yes, many. A man may have a foot in both worlds; he may be half in and half out; no one would call this an "abundant" entrance. Or a man might get through the gate with bruises; he might enter into the kingdom halt and maim. Or yet again, a man might be saved "so as by fire"; he might owe his life to leaving everything behind and beginning the new world as a pauper. All these have one thing in common; they each imply an entrance into the kingdom with a mutilated nature. Now, with every kingdom but that of Christ, this is *actually* the mode of entrance. There is no other instance known to me of "an entrance ministered abundantly." Does the Indian get an abundant entrance? No; he gets into the life of God by losing his individuality. Does the Egyptian get an abundant entrance?

93

No; he is fettered by the spot where his body lies. Does the Greek get an abundant entrance? No; he gives up his waking for a dream. Does the Mohammedan get an abundant entrance? No; there is only room in his paradise for the *outer* man. Does the Platonist get an abundant entrance? No; the inner man *alone* can enter there; there is no place for a child's toys. But in Christ's kingdom there is no mutilation. Death has no dominion over it. To reach it we do not even *wait* for death; its gate is here. When I enter that gate, I drop nothing; the whole man goes in—body, soul and spirit, without blemish and without blame. That is what I understand by the words, "Ye are complete in *Him*." By no other gate shall you enter complete. You are not complete in Plato, complete in Mohammed, complete in Buddha; you cannot enter *their* gates with praise, for you come in the poorer. But you are complete in Christ. He is the one Master that mutilates not, the one Master that gives an abundant entrance. He has a mission for every side of your nature—eye and ear, mind and brain, heart and soul. He has the crystal river and the new song and the unsealed mystery and the saintly communion and the endless activity and the ceaseless rest and the kingly power and the ministrant life. For what instinct of my nature has He not prepared a room!

Lord, I often speak of my "spiritual concerns." I speak as if a part of me were about to enter Thy kingdom and the other part were to be left behind. When I so think, I forget the abundance of Thine entrance. Teach me that every side of my being is a spiritual concern! Teach me that every gate may be the gate of entrance into Thy temple—the gate called Beautiful! Let my *wealth* be the Beautiful Gate—may I spend for the hungry! Let my health be the Beautiful Gate—may I work for the toiling! Let my manner be the Beautiful Gate—may I be gracious to the lowly! Let my voice be the Beautiful Gate—may I sing for the weary! Let my learning be the Beautiful Gate —may I grow humbler as I climb! Let my sight be the Beautiful Gate—in the glow may I see Thy glory! Let my hearing be the Beautiful Gate— in the wind may I catch Thy whisper! Let my heart be the Beautiful Gate—in the power of pity may I read Thy purpose! Let my pain itself be the Beautiful Gate—in sorrow may I trace the secret of human brotherhood! So shall heaven open by a hundred doors.

THE HUMAN HELP TO THE DIVINE

"Jesus saith unto her, Give me to drink."—JOHN IV. 7.

THERE was a man of my acquaintance who had once injured me, and from whom I had therefore been long estranged. Yet he had been linked to associations of my past, and I had a great wish to be reconciled. What course was open to me? Should I write a letter of forgiveness? That would be a form of accusation. Should I do him a favour? That would be coals of fire, and coals of fire are not agreeable to the recipient. I decided upon an opposite method. Instead of doing a favour to him, I would ask him to confer a favour on me. I did; he granted it, and resumed the friendship. And in that hour I understood for the first time the deep significance of the narrative of Samaria. Here is a woman whose life has been very bad; her spirit is in a state of enmity to Christ. Christ wishes to draw her heart into sympathy with His own. How shall He do so? He has all possible gifts at His command; shall He load her with His benefits?

96

The Human Help to the Divine

No. This woman is already in a state of spiritual pauperism. She has lost the sense of her own dignity, and benefits would perpetuate that loss. Christ feels that His favours would simply make her sore, accentuate her alienation, increase her dislike to holiness. Accordingly He who knew what was in man says: " Instead of helping her, I will let her help me; I will let her first sense of grace be a sense of rising dignity—a relaxation of the humiliating chain." He who came to minister asks this woman to minister to Him. He asks a drink of water. It was a very small boon; but the treasure lay in the asking, not the getting. The woman was uplifted in a moment. She would have *crouched* if she had been *offered* something; but to be asked for something—that was grand! That a poor creature like her should give a subscription to the Church Universal, that one of Christ's paupers should be requested to join a committee for the building of His Temple —this was exhilarating, this was reconciling, this made life *again* worth living! It was something to have answered a prayer of *Jesus!*

Lord, I often thank Thee that Thou hast heard my prayers; do I ever bless Thee that I have heard Thine! For indeed by day and night Thou prayest to me. I often speak of being awakened to spiritual life. What is it that has awakened me from sleep? Is it my prayers? No, Lord, it is Thine; I have heard a knocking at the door, and my slumber has been broken. It is *Thy* want which has broken my slumber—not mine. It is not I that have knocked at the door of *heaven*; it is Thou that has knocked at the door of earth. I am the child of *Thy* prayers—not my own. Samaritan as I am, sinner as I am, Thou hast asked drink of me. I am glad that Thou hast asked drink of me. I am glad that Thou hast allowed me to begin by giving, not receiving. To a heart crushed with sin, to a heart that has done nothing for Thee, Thy benefits are a load; they bring more weight than wing. But to benefit *Thee*—that is an *un*loading of my soul. To be waited on by Thee is the life of the invalid; but to *wait* on Thee is to renew my strength, to mount up on wings as eagles. There is no fragrance like that of my alabaster box—the box I break for *Thee*. There is no radiance like that of Bethlehem's gold—the gold I bring to Thee. There is no freshness like that of Samaria's water—the water I pour for Thee. I thank Thee, O Lord, that Thou hast asked something which is mine.

THE LAND WITH A GOLDEN TWILIGHT

"At evening time there shall be light."—Zech. xiv. 7.

Judah declination & hope

THIS is a promise made to the *nation ;* and as such it is unique in history. I do not mean that no nation but the Jew has ever predicted the glory of its advanced years. I know of none that has *not ;* every people glorifies its own future. But the peculiarity of this promise is, not that it glorifies the future, but that it glorifies the evening. The evening of a nation is its decline—the time when it has lost its political influence and its military prestige. To say that a nation shall have light at evening time is to say that it will be a power in its decrepit days, that in the period of its old age it will exercise the influence of the morning. That is the promise given to Judah, and it is unique. But there is something *besides* which is unique and whose uniqueness is more remarkable. This promise has been fulfilled. There may be disputes about other prophecies. There may be controversies about the interpretation of other predictions.　There may be difference of opinion as to whether a presaged glory refers to a Hezekiah or a Christ.　But this is a prophecy which is being fulfilled before our eyes.　We see one among the peoples of the world whose light has come only at evening time—in the hour of its decay.　Judah has indeed reached her evening shadows.　She has hung her harp upon the willows.　She has lost her local habitation.　She has been driven from her rites of worship.　She has been expelled from her temple.　She has been robbed of her prophet, her priest and her king.　She has been sent to sojourn in every land, and in none has she found a home.　Yet, in her darkness she is giving light to the world.　Never did she give such light as now.　Not when David sat upon her throne, not when Solomon swayed her sceptre, not when seer and psalmist sang her glories, did she give such light as now.　From the ruins of her battered tower she rules all nations.　From a ledge of her broken wall she gives law to the world.　From the places of her exile she dictates to modern civilisation.　From the scene of her blindness she illuminates the kingdoms by a torch she cannot see.　At her evening time there has been light.

Lord, these ancient people of Thine have seen their evening, but not their light.　They are dreaming still of a *future* glory—of a universal empire, of a kingdom which shall enfold all mankind. It never strikes them that the kingdom has come already. They deem themselves to be in bondage to the Gentiles; they wot not that the Gentiles are even now their subjects. They say, " We shall one day give a King to the world; " and lo, their King is already here—seated on His Throne, ruling from sea to sea! Show them, O Lord, their " light at evening time "! Reveal to them the radiance of their ruins, the empire of their evening sky! Teach them that the majesty of the Gentiles is the majesty of *their* Messiah! Tell them that our gardens are glorified by *their* flowers, our houses heated by their fires, our fields fructified by their corn! Tell them that we are living by their labour, fed by their fulness, braced by their breezes, enriched by their rivers, freshened by their fountains, strengthened by their struggles, inspired by the spirit of their life! Tell them that their King has come, that their fancy is fulfilled, that their empire is established, that their conquest is complete, that their mission is manifested, that their progress is perfected, that their world is won! Let them see their glory in the evening light!

THE BROAD WAY OF GOD

"Thine eyes shall behold a far-stretching land."—Isa. xxxiii.
17 (R.V.).

THE promise contained in these words is a
promise that the later religious life shall have
an expanded view. This is not our common
opinion of the religious life. The popular notion
is that the outlook should be widest at the
beginning, and should contract with advancing
years. The vision of religious breadth is supposed to belong to the young. But it is a great
mistake. Youth is the time for emphasizing
differences. It admits of no compromise. Whatever cause it takes up, it takes up sharply and
antithetically. When it takes up Christ it puts
Him on an island—with a sea between Him and
all things. It delights to think how narrow its
land is, how separate from all other lands. It
finds its glory in the dividing-line between Christ
and the world. It says : " The dance is incompatible with devotion, the evening party incon-
gruous with earnest piety." It bids the seeker

of Canaan abstain from the feast of Cana, the worshipper at Bethlehem recoil from the supper at Bethany; when it hears music in the Father's house it will not go in. But the advanced Christian feels very differently. He says, with the Seer of Patmos, " There shall be no more sea." The waters that encompass the island are dried up, and he beholds everywhere a far-stretching land. The Christian road has become an all-embracing road; it claims for Christ the spots it once repudiated. It plants the cross in the middle of the highway. We no longer say, " Six days for the world and one for God." The Sabbath has ceased to be an island. It has become connected with the mainland; it has given its *character* to the mainland. Instead of one day of rest, we would have rest in *all* the days. We would *work* by the Sabbath rest—the spirit of peace within. Between the Church and the market-place there is no more sea. There is an altar possible at the receipt of custom, an opportunity for sacrifice at the exchange, a chance for self-surrender at the counting-house, a sphere for Divine service in the haunts of commerce. In the completed life of Christ Heaven and earth are one far-stretching land.

Lord, hasten that happy time when between my

duties on Sunday and my duties on Monday there shall be no more sea! Give me an expanded view of what it is to be religious! Show me how far-stretching it is, how many things are included in it! Teach me that the road to Emmaus is broad enough to hold many travellers! The further I journey on that road, let me learn more how vast it is! Make my afternoon more charitable than my morning! Let me see how those can stand on *Thy* road that dared not stand on mine! Let me see into what unlikely quarter stretches Thy street of gold! Let me see there the leper that I loathed, the demoniac that I despised, the sceptic that I scorned, the fallen that I flouted! Let me see the child in spirituality whom I deemed unfit for my arena taken into Thine arms, the man who would not take Thy name accepted for Thy nature, the woman who had no creed chosen for a cry! The midday shall be more glorious than the morning, if only it reveals how far-stretching is Thy land.

AN IDEAL YOUNG MAN

"I have seen a son of Jesse the Beth-lehemite, that is cunning in playing, and a mighty valiant man, and a man of war, and prudent in matters, and a comely person, and the Lord is with him."—1 SAM. XVI. 18.

WHAT a magnificent assemblage of qualities! What element is omitted that can secure success! Here is personal attractiveness, "a comely person." Here is business-like sagacity, "prudent in matters." Here is athletic vigour, "a valiant man of war." Here is social accomplishment, "cunning in playing." Here, finally, is the spirit of religion, "the Lord is with him." The young man thus described is David. He is dowered from every direction—by nature, by art, by experience, by heaven. And yet, after all, the remarkable thing is not the number, nor even the variety of these qualities. What strikes me most is their seeming oppositeness. They are not the qualities which we should expect to find united. Personal attractiveness often interferes with prudence; we say, in common speech, that such a man gets his head turned. Devotion to art

[handwritten margin notes: "dowered from every David direction" and "Magnificent assemblage of qualities"]

naturally detracts from muscular vigour; the man of the study is not apt to be the man of war. Finally, such a blaze of human glory often obscures for a time the other world and holds a veil over the face of God. Is there anything that can unite these qualities, that can make them act in harmony? Yes, there is one thing which can; it is love. Love can join all these varieties. Love can make comely; it can kindle even a plain face into glory. Love can make strong; it can put valour in the heart and power in the sinew. Love can make prudent; the wisdom of the serpent may lie in the harmlessness of the dove. Love can make artistic; it is itself the very essence of beauty, the very soul of loveliness. And love can make religious; its thirst for the beautiful is not gratified below; its artistic eye seeks a better country. In love all fulness dwells.

Strong Son of God, Immortal Love, descend in Thy fulness upon the spirit of youth! Bring into the heart of our young men that union of qualities which, in Thine absence, are opposed! Give them the valour of the soldier—the strength that will not stoop to wrong! Give them the suavity of the courtier—the gentleness of manner which is ever comely! Give them a sense of beauty—a taste for all that is fair in literature and art, that life may to them reveal its romantic joy! Give them that with which a romantic joy is often incompatible—the spirit of prudence, a power of far-seeing, a judgment calm and clear! Give them, above all, a pious soul—a reverence for what is righteous, a hope for what is holy, a trust in what is true! Forbid that they should associate Thy religion with unmanliness! Forbid that they should say, "It is unheroic to ask help from heaven"! Teach them that Thy help makes heroes! Teach them that the leader of men is the leaner on Thee! Teach them that there is none so brave as he who lies on Thy breast, none so wise as he who bends to Thy will, none so courteous as he who has sunk self at Thy cross! Light them by the love of Thee! Thy love alone gives an all-round manhood. It has the courage for Calvary, the wisdom for temptation's wilderness, the manner for the marriage feast, the fervour for the fields of beauty. It is grave without gloom, free without frivolity, prudent without prudishness, pious without pretension, calm without coldness, winsome without weakness, trusty without truculence, winged with radiance and yet weighted with responsibility. Be ours Thy spirit of manhood, O Lord!

THE WELLS AND THE POOLS

"Who passing through the valley of Baca make it a well;
the rain also filleth the pools."—PsA. LXXXIV. 6.

WHEN a man is in the valley of tribulation he
may have consolation from two sources. He may
get it by activity, or he may get it by lying passive.
He may get a supply of water from a well which
his own hands have digged, or he may get that
supply from the pools which the rain has filled.
In the case of digging the well I work for my
consolation, in the filling of the pool by the rain
my consolation works for *me*; I have power to *dig a
well*, but the filling of the pool with rain is *Nature's*
deed—God's deed. Have you not experience of
these two consolations? Sometimes you get water
by your own digging—comfort by your own effort;
when a treasure is taken away, you think of the
gold still left to you. But there are other times
in which your comfort comes, not from the wells of
earth, but from the rains of heaven. And these, I
think, are the most frequent moments. I am not good
at digging wells when I am in the valley of Baca;

the heavy heart makes a weak hand. In my prosperous hours I use the wells more than the pools. But in my hour of adversity I am chiefly dependent on the pools. My digging power is small; I find it hard to brace myself by the remembrance of remaining mercies. If I had no resource but the digging of wells, I think I should die; the explanation of my continued life is the fact that " the rain, also, filleth the pools."

I bless Thee, O Lord, for these waters sent from *heaven!* I bless Thee for the strength that comes to me without my effort! Often has it come to me just when I had given up the digging— just when I had thrown away the spade in despair. When all my human doors have closed, an invisible door has opened, and there has come to me an incomprehensible strength, an unaccountable calm, an inexplicable peace. The water denied to the wells has appeared in the pools, and I am refreshed from above. In vain I ask the *earth* for the cause of my refreshment. There is nothing at my feet to explain it. The valley of Baca is a valley still. The ground is dusty and dry; my hands are too feeble to dig a well below. But when I look up it is all accounted for; Thy rain filleth the pools. Elijah was fed by ravens, but that was a *small* miracle! I have been fed by

Thee—directly, without a medium! The wells have been superseded by the pools. What the earth could not send up, Thy heaven has poured down. What the ground could not give, Thy grace has yielded. What human effort could not buy, Thy Divine love has granted free. My strength in the lowly valley has come from Thine upper air. I have not been left to the weariness of waiting for the *well*; Thy rain has also filled my pools!

THE DANGER OF TRIFLING THINGS

"Turn ye not aside, for then should ye go after vain things."
—I SAM. XII. 21.

THERE is a strange sense of anti-climax in
these words. Samuel tells the people not to turn
aside from God. This advice is very natural.
But the reason on which he bases it is rather
startling. He says that if men deviate from God
they will "go after vain things." It seems a most
lame and impotent conclusion. Why does he fear
emptiness so much? The departure from God is
ever to be deplored; but surely it is not to be
most deplored when it makes men shallow,
frivolous, vacant-minded! Are not these simple
things, harmless things, innocent things—things
to which we attribute the word "silly" rather than
"sinful"? Yet I think the prophet is right. Who
is the man furthest away from God—in other
words, who is the man whom it would take
longest to bring home? Is it he who has been
led astray by passion? Is it he who has fallen
into enmity? Is it he who has outraged his

113

conscience by a deed of evil? Not so; all these
have come back within a few days. Magdalene
has turned her own passion into the Lord's
Passion; Saul has changed his fire of enmity
into a fire of love; Peter has made his conscious
guilt his consciousness of glory—all these have
come home. But the great difficulty is to bring
back the unthoughtful—the men taken up with
the breadth of their phylacteries and the enlarging
of their garments. Simon the Pharisee is farther
off than Magdalene, for he is more vacant. What
is the extreme opposite of the calm sea? Is it
the stormy sea? No; any moment the storm may
become a calm. The extreme opposite of the
calm sea is the stagnant pool. Why so? Because
it lacks something which is possessed both by the
sea in its calm and the sea in its roughness—life.
There is no deterrent from God like the worship
of trifles, because that is an idolatry unaccom-
panied by a sense of sin. Trifles do not trouble
the conscience; and, where the pool of conscience
is untroubled, Bethesda has no healing spring.

Lord, save me from lifting up my soul unto
vanity! There is a pride which brings its own
fall. When I aim at impossible things I am
taught my presumption by stern experience. But
when I aim at things beneath me, I never learn

my need; my pride gets no fall. The lowness of my aim lulls me into a false rest. I lose my longings; I crush my cravings; I drop my desire for higher things. I mistake my passiveness for peace, my deadness for decorum, my lethargy for life. If I aspired to a Tower of Babel, my failure would confound me and perhaps redeem me; but I am satisfied with a house upon the sand, and my soul is unconvicted of sin. When Thou passest through my Galilee, I do not come to Thee. Greater sinners come—Zacchæus comes, Mary comes—but not I. Why is this, O Lord? It is because my infinite selfishness lies in so small a vessel. I have done no harm as Zacchæus has, as Mary has; it seems a small thing that I have done no *good*. I have placed my treasure in a trifle, and the trifle veils Thee from me. Rend that veil, O Lord! Show me the virulence of the poison in the tiny box! Break the box! Trample on the trifles! Cause the vain things to evaporate! Banish the baubles that keep me from school! Take away the toys that divert me from thought! Put aside the playthings that tempt me from reflection! Teach me to know my need of *Thee!*

THE RELIGIOUS STAGE BELOW
PRAYER

"I have looked upon My people, because their cry is come unto Me."—1 SAM. IX. 16.

WE often speak of God as the hearer and answerer of prayer. The Bible goes much further than that; it says He is the hearer and answerer of the cry. You will distinguish between a prayer and a cry; they are not the same thing. A prayer takes definite aim; a cry is a random shot. A prayer is the expression of a particular need; a cry may be the voice of a want unknown to him who utters it. A prayer is addressed direct to the ear of the Almighty; a cry may be addressed to no one, but may simply cleave the air. That God should answer my prayer is a very endearing thought; but it is more endearing still that He should answer my cry. There is a certain amount of *homage* in a prayer; there may be none in a cry. A cry may be purely secular. The cry spoken of in the passage was so. It was wrung out by a worldly sorrow. It was not so much prompted by longing for the future as by dissatisfaction with

—the present; the people groaned because they were weary of the Philistines. Yet God says, "Their cry is come unto Me." A very striking expression! I understand it to mean that the cry reached Him though it was not sent to Him; the value of a prayer was imputed to an expression of mere worldly want—to something which had "no language but a cry." And what was true of ancient Israel is true of modern England. For every single *prayer* that God hears He hears a hundred cries. Many who utter them would be called men and women of the world; yet God accepts their cry as a protest *against* the world. It is something to be weary of the Philistines! It is something to be unfilled with the swine-husks! It is something to feel that, when life has loaded me with luxuries, there is a great void left behind! That void is to my Father equal to a voice of prayer. The message has no address, but it comes to *Him*.

Lord, there was a time when men said of me, "He is not a man of prayer." They said, "He never lifts his voice to the Father of spirits; he is steeped in the cares of the world." They were wrong. They forgot that the cares of the world are cries, and that cries reach Thee as well as prayers. If I were at home in the world, I should have no care in the midst of its pleasures; they would fill me. But it is just in the midst of its pleasures that I have the deepest want. I never long so much for the wings of a dove as at the top of the earthly hill. It is then that my cry comes. Doubtless it is no prayer. It is not aspiration; it is only disappointed retrospect. But the disappointment makes it music in Thine ear. It tells Thee that I am too big for my toys. Thou hearest as yet no request; I ask Thee for nothing; I have not even called on Thee by name. But I have called on Thee by *need*. We speak of Thee as the hearer; Thou art more—Thou art the overhearer. Thou understandest my thought afar off—afar off even from myself. Ere I can speak a *word* Thou hast overheard my *cry*. Thou hast not waited for my asking, for my power to ask. Thou hast read in my groan more than I could say. Thou hast come, not to my voice, but to my void. Before I have learned to bless Thee, Thou hast seen my blank without Thee. Thou hast rated me above my present worth. Thou hast interpreted my cry as a creed, my sigh as a sympathy, my want as a wish, my poverty as a prayer, my discontent as a devotion, my lament as an accent of love. I praise Thee, O Lord, that Thou hast overheard the complainings which were not sent to Thee.

THE DIVINE IDEAL OF DOMINION

"The Lord's portion is His people; Jacob is the lot of His inheritance."—DEUT. XXXII. 9.

THERE is no possession of which a high nature feels so proud as the possession of a human soul. An inferior nature values above all things the ownership of houses and lands. But to a spiritual mind the greatest inheritance in the world is the mastery over another's spirit—specially over another's heart. We often use the expression, "My own one, my own dearest." At these moments we feel the sense of possession to be a peculiar luxury. We would not resign this particular kind of mastery for all the wealth of India and all the land of Canada. The sense of possession which says to a human soul, "My own!" is the climax of conscious power. Now, that is what I take the passage before us to mean. "The Lord's portion is His *people*"—not the mastery over stars and systems, not the control of storms and hurricanes, not the command of forces and thunderbolts, but the empire over human hearts;

117

this is the triumph of heaven, this is the power of God. Nor has the passage yet exhausted itself. If what God wants to possess is a human soul, what He wants most is a soul of the type of Jacob, "*Jacob* is the lot of His inheritance." Is not that a strange desire! Why such a type as Jacob! Why not Abraham or Isaac or Joseph! These were steadfast, unwavering men, never halting in the march, never weary on the way. But Jacob was a lame foot, ever stopping, ever sliding. Was he not a poor creature at the best—one of the waifs and strays that sleep on Bethel stairs, one of the flickering lights that struggle with the wind? Yes, and therefore he was worth conquering, worth possessing. Have you not read, "There is more joy in heaven over one sinner that repenteth than over ninety and nine which went not astray"? God's most precious inheritance is the sheep that wandered. To hold a fugitive heart, to master a wayward mind, to fix a changing fancy, to dominate a contrary desire, to captivate an escaping conscience, to win a stubborn will, to prostrate an ignoble passion, to soften a prodigal son—that is the inheritance in Jacob, that is the joy of the Lord!

Lord, let me gather for Thee these sons of Jacob! Let me gather for Thee these unlikely lives which seem impossible to mould! Let me gather them from the houseless and the homeless! Let me pick them up from life's Bethel stairs, from the pillars of stone to which sin has consigned them! Let me raise them from the bed of clay where an elder brother's wrath has laid them! Let me inspire their night with a dream—a dream of coming glory! Let me show them that a ladder may rise from the very stones of their humiliation! Let me show them that the pillows on which they lie may to-morrow be the steps of Thine altar! Let me tell them that, though they know not Thy name, Thou art wrestling with them every day! Let me teach them that Thy blessing precedes the daybreak, that Thy love is earlier than their light, that the striving of Thy Spirit waits not for their morning sunshine! Let me bring to them the tidings that Thou hast sought them before the dawn, greeted them ere the sunbeam smiled, struggled for them without a streak of day! So shall they learn that Thou art the God of Jacob.

THE SECRET OF ISRAEL'S GREATNESS

"Behold, I have taught you statutes and judgments; keep therefore and do them; for this is your wisdom and your understanding in the sight of the nations."—DEUT. IV. 5, 6.

I TAKE the idea to be that the greatness of the people of Israel was a moral greatness: "*This* is your wisdom in the sight of the nations." God has given to each nation a different kind of wisdom. He has given to China the spirit of order, to India the spirit of devotion, to Persia the spirit of religious struggle, to Egypt the spirit of reverence, to Greece the spirit of beauty, to Rome the spirit of empire. But Israel's one lamp is the love of righteousness. I do not think she has any love so strong as that. She has not arranged her household like China; her twelve tribes are scattered to the winds. She has no mystic moments like India; she seeks the things of common day. She has no religious doubts like Persia; her faith is a child's faith. She has no sense of eternity like Egypt; enough for her is the *earthly* promised land. She has no secular arts like Greece; she keeps her poetry and her music for the ear of God alone. She has no dream of personal conquest like Rome; if she seeks an empire, it is for Messiah. But, in one thing she is alone among the nations—her cry for earthly goodness. It is *earthly* goodness. She is not anxious how she will appear before the great white throne; she never speaks of that; she leaves that to Egypt. For her the question is, How shall I equip myself below?—shall I honour my father? shall I help my brother? shall I serve my neighbour? shall I comfort my friend? shall I be just in the exchange? shall I be fair in the market-place? shall I be true in the witness-box? shall I be pure at the family altar? These are homely questions, yea, they are problems of the home; but they are hers —hers alone, hers distinctly, hers by nature and birthright; *this* is her wisdom among the nations.

I thank Thee, O Lord, that amid the notes of the nations Thou hast prepared a place for " Home, sweet home." I thank Thee that in the great orchestra which sings Thy manifold beauty there is a place for the minor chords—the chords that vibrate to the dusty day. India has soared for Thee, Persia has fought for Thee, Egypt has dreamed for Thee, Greece has dressed for Thee; but is there to be none to walk for Thee? Among all the voices of the nations, is there to be none that shall say, " Lo, I come, I delight to do Thy *will*"? I thank Thee that there is *one*. I bless Thee that amid the sweet singers of this world there is one that sings in the street—sings the common song of duty. I praise Thee that among the birds of morning there is one which carols on the ground—warbles where men walk, trills where men toil, sings where men struggle with the hour. Thou hast given to Greece her music for the grove, and to Rome her music for the battle, and to Egypt her music for the funeral march of time. But I am glad that Thou hast added one strain more—a strain for the humble. I am glad that to one land Thou hast given the simple song, " Be just, be good, be true! " I am glad Thou hast a music for the market-place, a chord for the common-place, a warbling for the worker, a pæan for the prosaic, a hymn for household burdens, a song for domestic service, a light for manual labour, a stream for the sultry way. Such has been the mission of Thy people Israel.

GOD'S ARGUMENT AGAINST ASCETICISM

" I will not henceforth drive out any from before them of the nations which Joshua left when he died, that through them I may prove Israel."—JUDGES II. 21, 22.

" I WILL not *henceforth* "—after this time. *Up* to this time God had made life easy for His people. He had lightened the force of their temptations by isolating them from bad company —by driving out the idolatrous tribes which used to inhabit the land. But now God says, " I will make a change; I will let the bad company remain." The spectator would have said, " This shows there is no Providence in history; if there were, would God allow the tares to corrupt the wheat ? " But God Himself claims the seeming blot as a bit of the handwriting. He says that it is just for the *sake* of His people He lets the bad company remain, " that through them I may prove Israel." And have we not here a lesson for all time ? We all feel that the temptations of individual life grow deeper as the years roll. A

child has few temptations; it has too little sense of the value of things to be tempted by them. Childhood is the age of Joshua; it is sheltered from its foes. But as life opens, temptation comes. Youth's paradise has forbidden trees which are nevertheless revealed trees. The child may hide himself among the leaves of the garden; the young man dare not. Would you have it otherwise! Is there any father who does not wish to prove his son! Do you think a single Christian virtue could exist if the bad nations were expelled! Could there be faith without a cloud, patience without a delay, hope without a fear, strength without a struggle! The flowers of God are ripened by the frost. Charity comes in the chill; pity is born of pain; sympathy is woven by sorrow; courage is bred by conflict; love is revealed by the threat of loss. Grace, too, is a flower of the battle-field. God has prepared for His people not a desert, but a city. He would not be loved without rivals. He would not have you come to Him just because there is no other. He would be the chief among ten thousand. He would be the conqueror amid conflicting claims. He would be the chosen out of the million, the one attraction amid many meetings. That is why He drives not out the temptations of the soul.

God's Argument against Asceticism

Not in the desert would I serve Thee, O my God. I would not come to Thee simply because I have lost my world, because Thou hast driven out the old nations. I should like to give Thee a better proof of my love than that. Even human love has sighed to prove itself. It has longed for the presence of danger that it may reveal its power of sacrifice. Shall my love for Thee be less strong, O my Father! Shall all my thirst for chivalry be kept for earthly beings! Is there to be no more amongst us the spirit of that man who cried, " Lord, if it be Thou, bid me that I come to Thee on the waters "! Shall not my love for Thee, like Peter's, wish to *show* itself! Shall it have no romance in it—no longing to dare something, to brave something, to sacrifice something! Has not romantic youth dreamed of how it will plunge into the water to serve the object of its love! And shall I have no such dream of serving *Thee*! Shall the desert be dear because it is not dangerous! Shall the solitude be sweet because it is not sacrificial! Shall the hermitage be holy because it has no hard hours! Nay, my Father, give me *scope* for my love! Bid me that I come to Thee on the waters! Let me cherish the dream that youth delights in—the dream of devotion in danger! Let me seek Thee in the storm; let me wait Thee on the wave; let me find Thee 'mid the fires; let me bless Thee in the battle; let me praise Thee in Thy peril; let me help Thee in Thy heaviness; let me join Thee at Jerusalem; let me crown Thee in front of Thy cross! Drive not out the nations from before me!

GOD'S FAITHFULNESS IN THE CLOUD

" The children of Israel asked counsel of the Lord, saying,
Shall I go up against the children of Benjamin, my brother?
And the Lord said, Go up against him. And Benjamin
destroyed of the children of Israel eighteen thousand men."—
JUDGES xx. 23, 25.

THIS is one of the most singular statements I
have met with in the whole course of the Bible.
The people of Israel are exercised as to whether
they shall go up to battle. They ask counsel of
God. They ask it honestly, reverently. They
pour out their hearts in prayer for a revelation of
God's will. The answer comes, Go! Joyous at
the Divine approval, they march to meet the foe;
they are defeated. We can imagine their recriminations against God and religion. We are tempted
to join in these recriminations. Is this the value
of prayer! we say. Here is a band of pious men
who have asked, Shall we go? and received the
answer, Yes. And yet these men have not been
successful; they have lost the day. Methinks the
sorest part of that loss would be the seeming
failure of their God. To be defeated in an enter-

127

prise is a misfortune; but to be defeated after God has blessed me, to be defeated after God has bidden me go, to be defeated when I am only following the will of my Father—that seems more than a misfortune; it appears a wrong. But look again. Is every call from God a call to material *success*? Is there no such thing as a call to failure? What is that which God wants to perfect in us? Is it the sense of possession? No, it is the sense of sympathy. And how is sympathy made perfect? Is it by the number of my victories? Nay, it is by the number of my defeats. It is not my gains but my losses that make me human. The disciples on the Mount had both a triumph and a defeat; the triumph was the vision of glory, the defeat was the cloud which overshadowed it. Yet the cloud did more for them than the vision. The vision made them cold to their brother man; they wanted to live in mountain tabernacles above the stream of toil. But the cloud sent them down to the demoniac at the foot of the hill—down to the wail of the weary, down to the sigh of the sad. It tuned them into tenderness; it strung them into sympathy; it touched their chords with the echoes of human care. The glory would have stranded them; God made the cloud their chariot.

O my Father, Thy promise is not broken by the

blast. Often have I marvelled at the seeming failure of that promise. I have heard Thee say to Abraham in the watches of the night, "I will make of thee a great nation"; and when the morning came I have seen him in the fires of Mount Moriah. Yet these fires were to him Thy promise fulfilled. If Thou wouldst make of me a nation it can only be through pain. My heart is no highway for the nations till it runs through the path of thorns. My joys often *divide* me from my brother. My prosperity may repel him, my success may anger him, my year of jubilee may be his year of jealousy. But in the fires of Moriah he *calls* me brother. He comes to my cross. He bleeds at my bereavement. He weeps at my winter. He sighs at my setting sun. It is my *defeats* that have won my battles, O my Father. Thou hast promised me ten legions, and Thou hast sent me Calvary; but it is Calvary that has made the legions. My cross has fitted me for the crowd. I was apart from my brother till I walked the wave; but the waters made us one. I was alone on the road till I gained the Garden; but my sorrow became my city. It was *pain* that parted my garments among the multitude—Thou hast fulfilled Thy promise in a cloud.

WORSHIP IN THE PRACTICAL

"They departed into a desert place by ship privately; and Jesus, when He came out, saw much people."—MARK VI. 32 and 34.

HERE was an interrupted purpose of religious rest. The disciples follow Jesus through a private passage with the view of being with Him alone. Presently they find themselves, not in a quiet room as they expected, but in the midst of a vast and crowded hall where the wants of men and women clamour to be known. It seemed an obstacle thrown in the way of their piety. How sweet it would have been to be alone with Jesus, far from the madding crowd! Why are they not allowed to have their little hour of intercourse with the Master, undisturbed by the wheels of life! We of modern times have often asked the same question regarding ourselves. Often have we looked forward to the prospect of freedom from worldly care. We have said, I will get into private life and then I shall have more time for communion with the Spirit of Christ. And lo!

130

as we come out from the world, we find exactly what the disciples found. We find that the cares of the world have followed us into our retreat, that our life is as crowded as it ever was, that we cannot commune with a *solitary* Christ. Is this a sad experience? I do not think so. I do not believe that God wishes any man to feel himself alone with Christ. If he did feel himself alone, how could he have communion with Christ's Spirit! My fellowship with Christ is the sight of *His* fellowship. Peter wanted a solitary communion on the mountain-top: " Let us make three tabernacles—one for Thee and one for Moses and one for Elias." Where lay the sting of the proposal? In the wish to include Moses and Elias? Not at all; but in the wish to *ex*clude everybody else. A Christ upon a mountain apart, a Christ whose sympathy was limited to five communicants, a Christ who had no share in the labours of the common day—such was no object for reverence, such was no being to love. If any man seeks a Christ like that, God will immediately send over the mountain a cloud of human cares, and allow the breeze to bear up to the hilltop the cries of the demoniac on the plain.

Let me not think, O Lord, that Thy com-

Margin annotations: Solitary christ? — Exclusion — Cares of the world

munion is confined to the private hour! When I have come out from the secret passage into the crowded hall, let me not say I have parted from *Thee!* I once sought a place for silent prayer; I went to the desert to find it. And lo! when I arrived I could not get near Thee— the pressure of the crowd was so great. And I said, "Why in this world of time hast Thou allowed us so little leisure to prepare for eternity!" But now I understand it, O my God. It is because the preparation for Thine eternity is *not* leisure. Not in my moments of meditation do I mirror best Thy heaven. I meet Thee oftenest when I am in search of my brother. I never find so short a way to Thy New Jerusalem as when I am beautifying the streets of the Old. I have read that Mary asked the dead body of Thy Christ and found instead a living Lord. So has it been with me; I have found *Thy Spirit* when I have been helping *man's body.* Never have I seen Thee so clearly as when I was breaking bread to the hungry; never have I loved Thee so dearly as when I soothed a brother's pain. I sought the friendless children, and I discovered Bethlehem. I visited the humble homes, and I found Nazareth. I followed the tempter's track, and I met Thy wilderness. I helped the marriage feast, and I recognised Cana. I gladdened a dining-table, and I saw Bethany. I aided the fisherman's toil, and I stood by the Lake of Tiberias. I bore a neighbour's cross up the Dolorous Way, and I felt myself on the brow of Olivet. I thank Thee, O Father, that I did not find my desert.

THE SEEMING MOMENTS OF DIVINE NEGLECT

"He saw them toiling in rowing; He cometh unto them, walking upon the sea, and would have passed by them."—MARK VI. 48.

"HE would have passed them by." He made it appear as if He were bound on another errand, as if He had not come for the purpose of helping them. Why so! When human life is struggling, why should Divine help even *appear* to pass by! Is this a subject on which man should be left to doubt even for an hour! If God is our refuge and our strength in the day of trouble, why should He put on the disguise of one who is travelling to farther fields and who is bent on other business! My brother, it is the sublimest wisdom on the part of your Father. God is your very present help in time of trouble; but I do not think it would be good for you if He were *revealed* as "very present"—present in such nearness as to exclude your own efforts. We often say, in speaking of human charities, that any help is bad which precludes *self*-help. But it is just as true of the charities of Almighty God. Nay, His

134

almightiness makes it all the more essential that He should veil His presence. Your Father will not encourage spiritual pauperism. If you are on a stormy sea He will save you; but He will not save you as one saves a bale of goods. You are not a bale of goods; you are a man; and it is as a man He would save you. You have a spirit, and He wants the co-operation of that spirit. Your effort can add nothing to His strength, but it can add greatly to your own value; and it is your value that your Father wants to secure. That is the reason why He seems to pass by. He would like you to call Him. You cannot call Him if you see Him to be here already. Your cry requires the mist. If He would wake the spirit of prayer He must create the delusion of solitude; He must make it appear as if you were alone. Therefore it is that He makes as if He would pass by. He hides His nearness; He conceals His purpose; He veils the hand that already touches yours.

My soul, often have I heard thee say with Israel's prophet, "Verily Thou art a God that hidest Thyself!" And in this thou namest thy Father well. He is indeed a God that hides Himself; but His hiding is His brightest revealing. He has never come so near to thee as when He seems to pass by. It is always by night thy

Father seeketh thee—by night and by means of night. Not thus does He come to other creatures. He comes to the sun in light. He comes to the hill in gold. He comes to the plant in warmth. He comes to the bird in song. But not so does He begin with *thee*—He cometh to thee with clouds. Wilt thou complain that thine is not the fate of the sun or the hill or the plant or the bird? Then art thou complaining of thine own greatness. He comes to thee in the night because He desires to hear thy cry. Thou art the only creature that has a cry for Him. Nothing else would pine if He passed it by. The sun would not long for its light; the hill would not grieve for its gold; the plant would not weep for its warmth; the bird would not sigh for its song. But *thou* canst long for *Him*, thou canst grieve for Him, thou canst weep for Him, thou canst sigh for Him, O my soul. The night of other things brings no music to His ear; but thy night gives Him songs. It warbles thy want of Him. It hymns thy hunger for Him. It sings thy search for Him. It chants thy choice of Him. It notes thy need of Him. It preludes thy prayer to Him. It voices the void of thy heart *without* Him. It is no wonder that, with such treasures in thy night, thy Father oft should choose the night for thee.

PROVIDENCE IN THE COMMON-PLACE

"The Spirit said unto Philip, Go near, and join thyself to this chariot."—ACTS VIII. 29.

THE Spirit of Providence is always manifested in *joining* things. It does not work miraculously, but it causes separate things to work together. Here was a whole train of separate incidents. An Ethiopian sat in his chariot. He was on his return journey—his business was done, and therefore his mind was at leisure. Being at leisure, he began to read. Out of the many books with which he might have passed an hour he chose the Prophecies of Isaiah, and, as the place was a desert, he was not likely to be disturbed. But, on the road, the chariot happened to pass a man, and the man whom it passed happened to be a Christian missionary. Into the heart of the missionary there came an unaccountable impulse to run after the chariot. All the circumstances were against the Ethiopian stopping his horses. Why should he take up a pedestrian simply because he was so impertinent as to run after his

137

carriage! And then, the Ethiopian was reading; why interrupt his reading by taking in a total stranger! Everything said, Do not stop! But he did; and by that act all the separate rays were united. They came together in one providential beam. Taken by themselves, any one of them might have been an accident. A carriage on a lonely road with a man reading inside is a very common thing. A pedestrian running behind a carriage is a very common thing. A religious teacher in an obscure sphere is a very common thing. An individual studying a chapter of the Bible is a very common thing. The momentary stopping of a conveyance, is a very common thing. But when all these seeming accidents were united, the result was a startling providence—the Christianising of a kingdom.

Lord, Thy life-miracle to me is the great issue that comes from the union of trifling things. In the world of chemistry I can make a third substance by uniting two separate substances; Thine is the chemistry of *life*, O Lord. We go our separate ways, my brother and I. He takes the high road on his own errand; I take the low on mine. We meet at an unexpected turning; and, as the result, there is fulfilled, neither his errand nor mine, but Thine. And what in all this

Came together in a providential beam —

The christianising of a kingdom

The chemistry of life

Desert Road not purposeless

is Thy message to my soul? It is the reverence for the trivial. Can I ever again say that a desert road is purposeless? Can I ever again say that an obscure ministerial sphere is burial? Can I ever again say that the passing of a carriage is uneventful? No, my Father. Henceforth to me these shall all be possible *sacraments*. I shall uncover my head to them as I go by. I shall look with veneration on the rejected stones of life's temple. When my lot is cast in an obscure place I shall bow to the solitude; who knows but Thou shalt make that cloud my chariot! When I am interrupted in reading a chapter I shall not say, "The flesh warreth against the spirit"; who knows but my interruption may be Thy commentary! When I see but one man in my audience I shall not cry, "The mission has failed"; who knows but in that one there is secured the most crowded of all cathedrals! I shall build an altar to the commonplace; I shall reverence life's daily round. I shall tremble before trifles; I shall sacrifice to the small; I shall worship what the world calls worthless. Samaria's well may be Thy welcome, Simon's feast may be Thy fellowship, a broken box of ointment may bring beatitude to Thy heart; make me solemn in the secular, O my God!

Solemn in the secular

THE TRUE SPHERE OF FAITH

"They could not enter in because of unbelief."—HEB. III. 19.

IT is not an entrance into heaven that is here spoken of, but an entrance into earth. The writer is speaking of a *physical* Canaan, a land of *human* rest. I think we lose the significance of the words by not keeping this in mind. We always associate belief with the salvation of the soul; it is here made a provision for the well-being of the body— a qualification for success in life. And the remarkable thing is that it is recommended for the *entrance* into life. The common view is that we should gain belief by our earthly struggles. We think of youth as by right a time for doubt, for mental unrest. We picture the soul's progress as a search for God—its early years a battle-field, its midday a suspended judgment, its evening a crown of peace. Not thus thought the writer to the Hebrews. To him belief was for life's entrance, life's gateway. Instead of regarding the world as a place for struggling into the knowledge of God, he regarded God as a means of struggling into a knowledge of the world. He wished to *begin* earthly life with God—not to seek Him by the aid of candles, but to light candles by the aid of *Him*. And is he not right! Suppose a young man to say, " I am about to get married ; if I am happy in my married life I shall believe in God ; if not, I shall refuse to believe." Where lies the fallacy of such a test ? It is here—he throws into the sea half his capital before beginning the struggle of life. One half, at least, of his wedded happiness will depend on the use of that very spirit of religion which he has resolved in the meantime to tie up in a napkin. It will not do to begin the world *without* God, and say, when you trip, " This proves there is *no* God." It is like an invalid who insists on walking by himself to see if there is a couch ten miles off. He must have his couch before starting—he must *begin* with rest. It is not by experience we gain calm ; it is by calm we gain experience. The wings by which I rise must be fostered in the *nest*. The force by which I run must be nourished at the hearth. The strength by which I toil must be fanned by the peace of home. To tread the courts of man I must trust the course of God.

Lord, come to me on life's threshold, come to me in the morning hour ! Not when the day is far spent would I first meet Thee. It might help me for *another* world, but it would be too late for this. It is not enough for me to gain heaven; I must win earth. I know that the parting sigh of a dying thief may secure paradise; but what untilled ground it will leave behind! I know that even at evening time there may be light—that my heart may burn as I walk with Thee towards the setting day. But the burning is for a new day— not for this; the fire in my bush is no longer for the wilderness. I should like an earlier flame, O my God. Why should my heart wait for *Emmaus* to set it on fire! Why should it not be kindled at Jordan—kindled for the wilderness, kindled for the marriage feast, kindled for the weariness at Samaria's well! Is it not for earth I chiefly need my heart's burning! Why should I keep my faith in Thee for the days of heaven! Is it not here that it would most help me—here, where the streets are *not* of gold—here, where the gates are not of pearl—here, where the rivers are not crystal-pure! I wish Thee for warfare; I need Thee for night; I seek Thee for struggle; I prize Thee for privation; I want Thee for the hours of weariness; I crave Thee for the strength in conflict; I cling to Thee for the rainbow in the cloud. Experience may tarry for the noontide, but faith should come with the morning light.

Mean Surroundings

Earliest offence

THE DIVINE IN THE HUMBLE

" Is not this the carpenter, the son of Mary, the brother of James, and Joses, and of Judah, and Simon ? and are not his sisters here with us ? And they were offended at Him." —MARK VI. 3.

THIS is the earliest offence given by the Gospel ; and to my mind it is deeply suggestive, because I think it is still the earliest offence taken by each individual soul. What is the ground of complaint here spoken of ? Briefly stated, it is the homeliness of Christianity. Men refused to recognise a thing which grew amid such mean surroundings. Had Jesus claimed anything less than a Divine message there would have been no objection to His mean surroundings. Had He claimed merely the inspiration of human genius no one would have seen any contradiction in the poverty of His environment. For all human conditions the Jew prescribed toil ; he desired that every man should learn a trade, should live as if he had to earn his bread. But when he came to speak of man's relation to *God*, then changed the spirit of his dream. To him the attitude of God was ever one

143

of *rest*. His God lay in the secret place of His pavilion, with the curtains drawn, and the doors shut, and the windows deafened ; He could only work through His angels ; He must not soil His hands with mundane things. He who professed to be a Son of God must be a child of mystery. He must have nothing homely about Him. He must be all soul, no body ; all wings, no feet ; all poetry, no prose ; all heaven, no earth. And is not this also *our* first ideal of the Divine Life. In our moments of religious awakening we deny that morality is evangelical. We are offended when a preacher cries, " Salvation is goodness, work is worship, integrity is the service of God!" We say, " These are common things, homely things, things for the exchange and the market-place ; you will see them in Nazareth every day." Happy Nazareth !—I would, then, that all the cities were like thee ! Know ye not that God's mountain is man's valley ! What did Christ bless on the mount ? It was earth's homeliest flowers—humble-mindedness, sorrow for another's fall, good temper, wish to do right, slowness to revenge, imputing of pure motives, power to throw oil on troubled waters. These are the seven valley flowers which the Lord has blessed.

Be not offended at their lowliness, O my soul !

The Divine in the Humble

I have heard thee say, "Oh, these were only the virtues for beginners!" Not thus did thy *Lord* mean them. These valley flowers are carried to the top of the hill; it is there they are displayed. Why did He carry them up; why did He not bring thee down to the vale and show them as they grew? Just because He would have thee to know they were *not* beginner's flowers. Thinkest thou it is easy to be good in common things! There is no task for thee so arduous. It is easy to feel poor in spirit when thou art under the stars of God; but it is hard to feel so under the rebuke of man. It is easy to be meek in the presence of the wise; but it is hard to suppress thyself in the streets of Nazareth. It is easy to think charitably of those who walk on a plain *above* thee; but it is hard to think so in the rivalries of the exchange. It is easy for thy pride to make its peace with heaven; but it is hard to throw oil on the waters if thou art insulted by an earthly worm. Gather thy *valley* flowers! Take them up tenderly; care for them constantly; watch them right warily! Water them lest they wither; protect them lest they perish; fan them with heaven's air lest they fade and die! The flowers of Galilee shall be the flowers of Paradise; magnify thy Nazareth, O my soul!

UNCONSCIOUS CHRISTIANITY

"Then asked they him, What man is that which said unto thee, Take up thy bed and walk? And he that was healed wist not who it was."—JOHN v. 12, 13.

HERE is a man who is very defective in his answers to the catechism, yet who bears in his body the marks of the Lord Jesus. The schoolmaster puts to him the question, " What man is that which said unto thee, 'Take up thy bed and walk'?" He is speechless. He is absolutely without a theology. He can give no account of Jesus—who He was, where He came from, whither He was going. Men would have said he was an agnostic; he "wist not." Yet, all unconsciously to himself, this man was already a Christian. He had bathed in the crystal fountain; he had felt the sparkling spray; he had experienced a new life in heart and limb. He was a disciple without knowing it—a follower without a faith, a convert without a creed, a devotee without a doctrine. If you had asked him what church he belonged to, he would assuredly have answered, " I am member of no church "; I do not know of

146

any communion that would have received a man of such limited knowledge. Yet at that very moment his name was certainly enrolled among the members of the Church Invisible. He was one of the hundred and forty-four thousand. He was numbered in the census of the New Jerusalem. He was a singer in the Choir Celestial; but he knew not the song he was singing. He was a painter in the Gallery of Grace; but he saw not the forms he was weaving. He was a builder of the Church Universal; but he thought he was making only a place for *men* to dwell in. He was led by the hand of Jesus; but he thought it was a servant's hand.

Lord, there are many men of Bethesda among Thy people still. There are those who, like Jacob, get a blessing from Thee before they have learned Thy name. Often have I figured to myself that little child whom Thou didst raise in Thine arms. It got the blessing before it received the teaching. Many there be who enter into Thy temple by that door. They serve Thee ere they can name Thee. Like Abraham, they walk in the Promised Land and think themselves elsewhere. They do not know the cause of their own hearts' burning. They say, "I got it from the torch of Nature; I was walking on the road to

Emmaus, and a man met me and gave me light."
Thou art that man, O Lord. It is Thou who
disguisest Thyself in the dress of common day.
It is Thou that meetest us on the secular road,
the Emmaus road, the road of those who
think they have abandoned Thee. It is Thou
whom we take to be the gardener; it is Thou
whom we mistake for the stranger. Often do we
say to a wayworn traveller, "Abide with us, for
it is evening, and the day is far spent." We call
the deed our philanthropy, our humanity, our
natural charity. And, all the time, it is prompted
by Thee. It is *Thou* whom I have asked to abide
with me. It is Thou whom I have sheltered from
the night. It is Thou whom I have constrained
to come in and rest awhile. My charity has been
chimed by Thee; my pity has been plumed by
Thee; my heart has been heated by Thee; my
kindness has been kindled by Thee; my compassion has been created by Thee. My benevolence is Thy blessing; my philanthropy is Thy
flame; my grace is Thy gift; my love is Thy
light; my mercy is Thy mediation; my sympathy
is Thy sacrifice; my tenderness is Thy tending;
my warmth is the working of Thy wings. I have
sought my brother by the footprints left by Thee,
and I wist not that they were Thine.

THE GOAL OF ADVERSITY

"He took her by the hand and lifted her up, and immediately the fever left her; and she ministered unto them."—MARK I. 31.

MARK had a very active mind—the most active mind of all the four evangelists. He delights to record not words but deeds. I do not think that any of the others, after telling of this woman's cure, would have immediately added, "and she ministered unto them." The sequel is not what we should expect. When an invalid awakes from the prostration of fever we expect to hear that others minister to *her*—do what they can to repair the ravages of disease. The first thing Matthew records about the convalescent daughter of Jairus is the command of Jesus that "something should be given her to eat." No doubt the time came when she also ministered to the household; but Matthew does not pass on to that; he drops the curtain at the couch of the invalid. Is Mark, then, less sympathetic? Is it want of sentiment that makes him haste to tell us how soon this woman

149

was up and at her work again? No; I think it is
the opposite feeling. Mark feels that the great use
of a temporary personal burden is the power it
gives for human ministration. This is a side of
the subject which we do not often look at. We
seldom view our invalid moments as preparations
for increased activity. But Mark does so view
them; to him this is their glory. The woman
raised from the bed of fever is not merely restored;
she is magnified. She is in a better state than if
she had never been ill. The illness has been an
enrichment. I think her new ministrant attitude
must have been to her friends as great a surprise,
as great a miracle, as her cure. They saw her,
very likely, as they had never seen her before—
lending a helpful hand with a cheerful spirit. But
to us of later years this will be no surprise. We
have learned something—the very lesson which
Mark meant to teach us—that pain is the ivory
gate and golden which leads into the heart of our
brother.

My soul, it was by the gate of the temple called
Beautiful that the lame man was laid; in the
moments of thine impotence, remember that.
Remember that thine experience of the cross is
itself the gate into the temple of sympathy. I do
not say it is thine only gate into *Heaven*; Heaven

Goal of Adversity

—many mansions. Thou shalt
... training here what shall be thy
...Perhaps thine is here an inquir-
...are yonder those who "inquire
...Perhaps thine is here the gift of
...are yonder those who "in His
...His glory." Perhaps thou hast
here the spirit of an artist; there are yonder those
whose temple is a place in which "to behold the
beauty of the Lord." But it may be that here thy
lot is simply to lie low—to be prostrated on a bed
of pain. That battered gate is the most beautiful
of all. It is thy training for the night service. It
is thy school for learning the art of mercy. The
barrier that chains thee is a rudimentary wing;
one day thou shalt fly with it. One day it will
bear thee on errands of love. One day it will
carry thee to the spirits in prison that thou mayst
lead them to fountains of living water. One day
thou shalt open more doors than the angels,
because thou hast been where they have not—in
the valley of tribulation. In the hour thou callest
death Christ shall take thee by the hand, and on
the wings of thine earthly infirmity thou shalt arise
and minister.

THE LIMIT TO DIVINE RETRIBUTION

"I will correct thee with judgment."—JER. XLVI. 28 (R.V.).

THE love of a good father is as much seen in his punishments as in his rewards. We all recognise the truth that the reward given to a child should be on the lines of the child's nature. No father would recompense a boy of seven by giving him a copy of Matthew Henry's Commentary; we should call that a reward without judgment. But parents do not so often recognise the fact that a child's penalty should be *also* on the lines of his nature, that he should not be *corrected* without judgment. A boy transgresses on the Sabbath day; you send him to write out the hundred and nineteenth psalm. What is the objection to this? It is too much, you say. That is not the objection; the evil does not lie in the quantity. It is not that the penalty is too much, but that it is too inappropriate. It is actually *helping* the child's heart to transgress against the Sabbath; it is fomenting his dislike of religious ordinances in

152

general and of the Bible in particular; it is a
correction without judgment. A girl tells you a
lie through fear; you lock her in a dark room.
Is that a wise correction? No; you are develop-
ing that very element which has caused her to
err—the overmastering power of fear. Or, instead
of the dark room, you confront her thenceforth
with a perpetually dark countenance—a face
which says: "You know I can believe nothing
from *you!*" Is that correction wise? No; it is
telling her she is measured by a low standard;
and when she realises that, she will soon come to
measure *herself* by a low standard. Never tell a
child that you expect nothing from him; that is
the way to *get* nothing. At the time of the flood,
never forget to show the rainbow, for the rainbow
is never so needed as then. It is in the hour of
penalty that we need the promise. Innocence can
dispense with vision; Eden can bloom without
prophecies; but the heart of fallen Adam must
be cheered with the prediction of the serpent
bruised.

There is always a light in Thy valley, O Lord;
Thy correction is ever tempered with judgment.
I have heard that every sin deserves Thy wrath
and curse. No, every sin deserves Thy penalty
and Thy promise. The stroke and the star, the

retribution and the rainbow, the pain and the pity, the smiting and the smile—that is what my erring soul requires. Thou wilt never send the stroke without the star, the smiting without the smile. The famine and the swine-husks *alone* could not send the prodigal home; it required the attraction of Thine eye—the eye that followed him when he was yet afar off. The pain of my sin comes not from the rod, but from the rose— the "awful rose of dawn." I cannot feel my chain till I hear the voices of liberty. It is when I see in the distance the warm fire of Thy love that I learn how cold I am. It is from Thy sun-beams that my stripes must come. Nothing but light can lash my sin. Nothing but beauty can burn my corruption. Nothing but revelation can rend my heart. It was when he saw Thy look of love that Peter wept bitterly. My sin can only be punished by a sense of Thy mercy; correct me by Thy mercy, O Lord!

THE FAITH PRECEDING EVIDENCE

" Faith which worketh by love."—GAL. v. 6.

I TAKE the words to mean that there are things
for which love is *itself* the evidence. There is a
familiar saying, " Seeing is believing." But it is
equally true that " feeling is believing." There
are some in this world who love because they
believe; but I think there are a still larger number who believe because they love. It has always
seemed to me—though it is not the common
opinion—that St. John belongs to the first class
and St. Paul to the second. John's motto is,
" Believe, and live "; Paul's motto is, " Live, and
believe." John sees the transfiguration glory and
then lies upon Christ's bosom; Paul lies upon the
bosom and is then caught up to see the glory.
John says, " If we walk in the light we shall have
fellowship"; Paul cries, " If ye be rooted and
grounded in love ye shall be able to comprehend,
with all saints, what passeth knowledge." I have
seen two children, each animated by perfect trust
in an earthly father, but each for a different reason.

The one virtually said, "I trust him because he loves me"; the other said in effect, "I trust because I love *him*." Now, I think the larger number of the human race belong to the latter class. The amount of faith we repose in others is quite disproportionate to our *knowledge* of them. You will see two girls in the course of a few hours becoming mutual confidants. Why is this? It is because they have taken a liking for one another. Their faith in each other has had nothing to work upon but love. There has not been time for experience. Love is the *anticipator* of experience. Love pays in advance; it gives the money before it receives the thing. Divine love is no exception. God pays man in advance for services not yet rendered; I suppose that is what the prophet means when he cries, "Behold! His reward is *with* Him and His work *before* Him!" Love gives its confidence in advance. It waits not for proof. It lingers not for corroboration. It suspends not its trust till its object is weighed in the balance. It surrenders its faith unpaid for.

My brother, be this thy faith in thy fellow-man! Do not wait till thou hast proved him! Thou lookest abroad upon the lapsed masses; thou seest no beauty to be desired in them. Wilt thou then let them go? Is thy faith to be dependent on sight? Not if thou lovest. If thou lovest thy lapsed brother thou wilt hope all things for him. Love gives the benefit of the doubt to those who seem unpromising. Love imputes its own righteousness to those who are still in shadow. Love believes in to-morrow for those in a dark to-day. My brother, if thou lovest, thou shalt believe that all things are possible for man. Though as yet thou seest no rainbow, though as yet thou hearest no bells across the snow, though as yet there has come from the waters not even an olive branch of peace, still thou shalt believe. Love itself shall be thy rainbow; love itself shall be thy bell of hope; love itself shall be thy message from the flood. Humanity is still climbing the Dolorous Way — fainting beneath her crosses, groaning amid her thorns. Wait not till she has conquered, wait not till she is crowned! Go out to meet her in her climbing! Go out to greet her in her night! Go out to own her in her rags! Take up her bitter cross and call it thine! And if men say to thee, "Why darest thou to hope for these withered leaves?" lay thy hand upon thy heart and say, "Love believeth all things!"

THE SUCCOUR OF THE TEMPTED

"In that He Himself hath suffered, being tempted, He is able to succour them that are tempted."—HEB. II. 18.

How can the writer to the Hebrews say this when he himself tells us that Christ's temptation was "without sin"? Is not the absence of sin the absence of a most important element for a sympathiser with human weakness? No, it is not. The soreness of a temptation, in my opinion, never lies in the presence of sin; it lies precisely in the concealment of sin. If the sin of the act were conspicuous, there would be very little struggle. The struggle of the temptation lies in the *hiding* of the evil. Temptation did not come to Jesus as a choice between good and evil—I do not think in its sorest form it comes to any man as a choice between good and evil. What we struggle with is a masked form, and we struggle to unmask it. The tempter tells Jesus that certain drastic acts will be for the good of the kingdom. In that motive lies Christ's temptation; His whole struggle is to discover whether the drastic act

158

would really be for the good of His kingdom; when He decides that it would not, the soreness of the temptation is gone. We have not all such high motives for listening to the tempter; but we have always a higher motive than the intrinsic love of sin. When we are tempted to do wrong our danger lies in the *eclipse* of sin—just as Christ's danger lay in His actual sinlessness. The succour we need is precisely the same as the succour He needed. We want to be shown that the course proposed would be evil; our cry is, " Show us the tempter, and it sufficeth—sufficeth to make us flee! " It is because Christ can do this that He is able to succour.

Jesus, when I go up to the mount of temptation, let it be with *Thee!* I am bound to go up, even as Thou wert. Often have I thought of these words, " Jesus, being full of the Holy Ghost, was led by the Spirit into the wilderness." Yes, it was Thy spiritual ecstasy that made the wilderness inevitable to Thee. It is my spiritual ecstasy that makes *my* wilderness inevitable. It is after my exaltation that my reaction comes. It is the very glory of my baptism that brings my desert. The sight of the open heavens makes me scorn the slow methods of earth. I am tempted to follow new paths, quicker paths—to be restive under the

old régime. Succour me, O Lord ! Succour me
as Thou Thyself wert succoured—by a vision of
the sin beneath the seeming good ! Show me that
the old régime is the Will of the Father, that the
new method is my own will ! Unmask the seeming
sanctity of sin ! Disrobe the tempter of his
trappings of truth ! Draw aside the veil from the
face of evil ! If I could see that face, temptation
would die. Reveal it, O Christ ! Thou alone
canst reveal sin.   Nothing but purity can disclose
impurity. It is written, " In Thy light shall we
see light " ; yea, but it is also true, " In Thy light
shall we see darkness." Shine, and I shall know
what night is ! Sing, and I shall know what discord is !   Speak, and I shall know what silence is !
Touch, and I shall know what solitude is ! Inspire, and I shall know what meanness is !
Quicken, and I shall know what death is ! Reveal
sin by the brightness of Thy coming, and I shall
yield to temptation no more !

BLEMISHES IN THE GREAT

" Then Daniel was astonied for one hour."—DAN. IV. 19.

THE words to my mind are strongly dramatic. They are meant to convey the impression of a contradiction in terms. Daniel at a loss even for one hour! Daniel at sea! Daniel at the end of his resources! It seems the climax of impossibility. For one hour of his life Daniel falsified his character—was found paralysed in judgment. Is it not a pity that God allowed it! Is it not a pity that man recorded it! Do we not love to think of Socrates as never having lost his temper! of Cæsar as never having lost a battle! of Solomon as never having lost an opportunity! Why should the Bible have allowed one rent to appear in the seamless robe of Daniel; is it not a breach of Divine art? I do not think so. I hold that nothing brings out moral beauty like a shadowy background. What a charming light is thrown upon Daniel's wisdom by this one hour of perplexity! It shows that his wisdom was the result of personal struggle—that it was not the wisdom of the bee or of the spider or of the ant—imposed from the outside, but that it was something to which, through darkness, he had to work his way. Men talk of the examples of the great; I think the finest part of their example is the one hour in which they fail. That one hour makes them *possible* for me. Before it, I looked upon them as specially endowed, raised by nature far above the reach of my hand. But that hour said: "Go and do thou likewise!" It told me that he whom I admired was a man of like passions. It told me that he, as much as I, had the element of human weakness. It is not the powers, but the difficulties, of the great that inspire us. I get my wings from their night—not from their sunshine. I make their clouds my chariot. I rise upon the step on which they fall. It is not the footprints they have left on the sands of time that impel me to follow; it is the spots where the footprints fail. Jacob may be a prince that has power with God; but he only becomes my example when he halts upon his thigh.

I thank Thee, O Lord, that Thou hast revealed in the life of each saint one dark hour. I used to wonder. It seemed a strange thing that the temple of a holy life should have one gate *not* beautiful. I do not wonder now; I adore the

162

wisdom that has made it so. I bless Thee, my
Father, for the saint's broken gate; it will be the
only gate of entrance for *me*. How can I aspire
to pass into the temple by his gate of glory! I
dare not mount with Elijah in his chariot of fire—
I should grow giddy with the height; but he had
an hour of despondency when he cried like a child;
I will meet him *there!* I dare not climb with
Moses to the summit of Pisgah—I am not fit to see
the Promised Land; but he had an hour of
temper when he showed the common clay; I will
meet him *there!* I dare not seek with Abraham
the top of Moriah's hill—I am not yet ripe for the
sacrifice; but he had an hour of trembling when
he chose the coward's part; I will meet him *there!*
I dare not fly with John to the visions of Patmos
—mine eyes would be blinded with the glow; but
he had an hour at Samaria when he forgot the
vision of his Lord; I will meet him *there!* I will
take wing from their weakness; I will get robed
from their rags; I will rise from the spot where
they wrestle; in the place where they flagged I
shall be constrained to fly. I thank Thee, O Lord,
for Daniel's impotent hour.

THE CHRISTIAN VICTORY OVER SORROW

"He saith to the sick of the palsy, Arise, take up thy bed, and go into thine house."—MARK II. 10, 11.

THIS man was made to reverse his relation to his former cross. He had been a paralytic. He had been brought to Jesus on a bed. His bed was his cross, and his cross had borne him down. But when he had met Jesus, instead of the bed taking up *him*, he took up the bed! His earliest strength was manifested in the lifting of that which had once weighed him down! One would have thought that a man who had just got rid of his cross would have *run* from his cross, would have left it on the highway and fled. Not so this cured paralytic. He *embraces* the emblem of his former pain—he carries his bed! So will it ever be with the Christian. He will not scorn the calamity from which he has been emancipated. He will not deem that his calamity was a loss of time. He will say, " I have got rid of it to-day because it is no longer my *portion* for to-day; but I still believe

164

it was my portion for yesterday." And because he feels that the cross was good for his yesterday, he will take it up tenderly after his cure. He will bear it into his house and keep it there—keep it as a memory. That is the difference between Christ and other masters. They, as well as He, profess to lift you from your bed; but they consign the bed itself to oblivion. Theirs is the gospel of extrication; it offers to cast your cross into the sea. But His is the gospel of vindication; it defends your cross in the very act of removing it. It bids you *take up* the bed on which you were lying. It tells you to carry it home, to make it a part of your furniture, to claim it as an item of your household riches. To triumph in Christ is not simply the *abolition* of pain but the transformation of pain—not merely the *death* of sorrow but the turning of sorrow into joy. Others may promise instead of a cross a crown; with Him the cross is *made* the crown. Others may promise to transport you from a valley into a mountain; with Him it is the valley itself that has to be exalted. Others may promise to remove all obstacles from your path; with Him it is the crooked things themselves that are to be made straight and the rough places themselves that are to become plain. Others may say, " Arise, and forget thy bed;"

165

with Him the mandate is, "Arise, take up thy bed and walk."

Lord, I have heard men say, "Go, bury thy sorrow." Yet methinks the peace which *Thou* givest is deeper than that. I could bury my sorrow without *Thee.* I could bury it in the wine-cup. I could bury it in the excitement of a cause. I could bury it in a withered heart. I could bury it in a winter of old-age whose snows benumbed the sense. The *world* could give my sorrow decent burial if that were all I needed. But that is not all I need. It is not forgetfulness of my cross that I most require; it is glorified remembrance. I want my cross not to be buried, but to be lifted up—raised into the sunlight. The world cannot do that for me, O Lord. It can say, " Bury thy sorrow," but not, " Take up thy bed." *Thou* canst say, "Take up thy bed." Thou canst show me not merely the burial of my cross, but its resurrection into newness of life. Thou canst transform my thorn into a flower. And I want my thorn transformed into a flower. Job has got the sunshine after the rain; but has the rain been all waste ! Job wants to know, and I want to know, if the shower had nothing to do with the shining. And Thou canst tell me — Thy cross can tell me. Olivet is not the death of Calvary; it is Calvary in bloom. Thou hast not buried Thy

The Christian Victory Over Sorrow

sorrow; Thou hast crowned Thy sorrow. Be this my crown, O Lord! The world can dry my tears, the world can drown my cares; but I only triumph in *Thee* when I have learned the radiance of the rain.

RELIGIOUS JOY

" Bear no burden on the sabbath day."—JER. XVII. 21.

DID you ever ask yourself why the Jew forbade
work on Sunday? It is commonly thought that
the prohibition originated in his gloomy views of
religion—in his tendency to regard worship as a
penance. I believe the motive was just the
opposite. I think the design of the command
was to associate the Sabbath with brightness.
Wherefore is it said, "Bear no burden on the
Sabbath day"? Is it meant to suggest a privation? No, it is intended to convey a privilege—
the sense of a holiday. The Jew associated his
Sabbath with the absence of a burden. He
associated it with leisure of mind and freedom of
body. He linked it with the idea of pleasure, he
bound it to the heart with a thread of gold. It is
as if he had said: " Let your Sabbath be a
happy day, a burdenless day, a flowery day. Let
it be a day when you will have a sense of release
from toil, of freedom from worry, of emancipation
from care. Let it be a day from which gloom

168

shall vanish, in which joy shall reign. Let it be a day for the birds to sing, for the brooks to warble, for the sunbeams to play. Let men think of God's presence as an hour of revelry, as an abandoning of care, as a release from the trammels of the school. Let them receive God's Kingdom as a little child receives its toy."

Forbid, O Father, that I should ever associate Thy service with a burden ! I shall never serve Thee well till the burden is fallen from me, till it is buried in the sea. As long as Martha is cumbered, she works badly. My soul is unlike a steamship ; it only goes rapidly when it is without effort. I am never quite active till I am passive— unresisting in Thy hand. If I am to serve Thee, I must be captivated by Thee. Take my heart captive, O Lord, and it will be free. I speak of my Sunday duties, of my religious responsibilities. These are not the words of love, of the captivated heart. Shall the lark meditate on the duty of its morning song ! Shall the child say, " My father will be angry if I do not ask him for a holiday " ! It is not the sense of *duty* I would cultivate ; it is the sense of privilege. Why should my heart be the only creature which does not *sing* in its element ! Thou art its element, O God ; why does it not sing in Thee ! The lark's element is

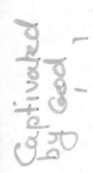

Captivated by God

Passive and unresisting in God's Hand

the morning, and it trills in the morning. The nightingale's element is the shadow, and it sings in the shadow. The fish's element is the sea, and it leaps in the sea. The ox's element is the meadow, and it browses in the meadow. But *I* never leap before the Beautiful Gate of my temple, O Lord; I seek the dirge instead of the dance, the silence instead of the song. When shall I be caught up to meet Thee in the air? When shall I repair to Thee as the hart repairs to the water-brooks? When shall I seek Thy tabernacles as the swallow seeks her nest? When duty shall be merged in love, when law shall melt in privilege, when service shall find that it is free. *Then* shall the burden fall from the Sabbath day.

THE WAY TO THE ALTAR

" Build thou the walls of Jerusalem! Then shall they offer bullocks upon thine altar."—PSALM LI. 18, 19.

IT is when the Jerusalem of the heart is built up that the heart offers its best sacrifice. We are all in a delusion about this matter. We tend to think that the hour of sacrifice is the hour of depression—that we give most when we are most wretched. The psalmists of Israel—the most devotional set of men that ever lived—are of a different opinion. Listen to the writer of the forty-third Psalm: "O send forth Thy light! then shall I go unto the altar." The world would have said, "Send me Thy *cloud;* let it bring me to Thine altar of sacrifice!" But Israel's singer knows better. He feels that the heart is most ready to outpour itself when it is basking in the sun, that it is most generous where its atmosphere is most genial. And indeed our deepest experience will cry, "Amen!" When do you bring your most precious gifts to the altar? It is when there is sunshine in your soul. I do not say it is when

171

there is sunshine before your *eyes;* the Cross of Calvary would prevent me from saying that. But if you want to offer a perfect sacrifice, you must have sunshine in your *soul.* Jesus had; He spoke of His peace, of His joy. The writer to the Hebrews says that He endured the cross and despised the shame " for the joy that was set before Him." The despairing heart is never the sacrificial heart. When the windows of your own spirit are darkened, you cannot look *out.* You hear not the cry of distress in the street; you see not the squalor in the lane. You do not seek out cases of need. You give your subscription when you are asked for it, but you give it mechanically— because to refuse costs effort. The coin in the hand of care is thrown down carelessly. Depression cannot work either for self or others. It wants to lie still, to be undisturbed. It evades a duty; it postpones a visit; it defers a letter; it delays an engagement; it declines an invitation; it resists whatever would force it to open the window. My sacrifice is born of my hope. It is when sitting by my own fire that I feel my brother's cold. If you would bring Jerusalem to the altar, you must first rebuild her walls.

Lord, it is for *sacrifice* I want joy. If I ask Thee for prosperity, it is not that I may fare

sumptuously every day; it is that others may fare sumptuously. If I ask Thee for light, it is not that I may bask in the sun; it is that others may bask there. I would feel my yoke easy and my burden light in order that I may help to their rest the labouring and heavy-laden. Send me not to a brother's sick-bed when my own heart is sick! Is it not written of the ministering spirits: " These are they that come *out* of great tribulation "? Bring me out into the day ere in Thy temple I serve by night! Set my feet in a large room ere I enter within the strait gate of the sorrowful! Show me the unconsumed bush ere I tread the desert of the lonely! Give me the grapes of Eshcol ere I visit the wards of the infirmary! Deck me with flowers of hope ere I sit by the couch in the hospital! Sing me the songs of *Zion* ere I meet with the sigh of the sufferer! I would see my risen Christ *before* I go into Galilee. I would break the bread *before* I climb my brother's cross. I would be led by the green pastures and laid by the quiet waters *before* I am asked to journey in the shadow of another's valley. I shall approach Thine altar of sacrifice when Thou hast rebuilt the walls of Jerusalem.

THE ILLUMINATING POWER OF THE SHADOW

" In the shadow of the branches thereof shall they dwell."—
EZEK. XVII. 23.

WHY in " the shadow " of the branches ? Why
not rest on the branches themselves ? Would not
such a foothold be an adequate sense of safety for
a human soul ? Yes—too much sense of safety.
It is not desirable, even for the pleasures of life,
that there should be no memory of shadow. How
often we are told that we ought to realise our
privileges. What does that mean ? Simply this,
that we ought to look at the shadows around us.
To realise our privileges is to consider the
possibility of another state of things. It is not
every prosperous man that appreciates his
prosperity. I think, to appreciate my prosperity
I must see a shadow. There is a phrase often
used in colloquial language, " You do not know
you are born." It is commonly spoken by
struggling people to those who are supposed to
have no struggle. Well, if there be any who
"do not know they are born," they are of all men

most miserable. They are like guests at a splendid banquet who have no sense of physical taste; they are like spectators of a lovely scene who have no sense of beauty. If you would teach me my light, you must bring me under the shadow. " What would you do without her ? " is a question which was once put to me concerning a very near relative. It was the invitation to imagine a shadow. And I think it was the suggestion of that shadow that first wakened me to the worth of my possession. I saw its glory in my imaginary gloom; I learned its riches by my fancied poverty. And ever shall I bless the day that placed in my sunshine the image of a possible shade. It has made me, not relax—as some would think—but intensify, my hold. It has deepened my sense of the light and my desire to keep it for ever.

My brother, always carry the shadow beside the glory !—not to dim the glory, but to make it more dazzling. Not by sunlight canst thou test the value of thy gold; thou must behold it by the shades of evening. At thy warm fire, remember that there are hearths which are cold! On thy downy bed, remember that many a Jacob has his pillow of stone! At thine ample board, remember that the beggar Lazarus is still sitting at the gate!

Thoughts for Life's Journey

In thy circle of home affections, remember the Abrahams to whom it is said, "Get thee out of thy country and from thy kindred and from thy father's house"! Say not that the shadow will obscure the shining; it is the shining that is obscured without the shadow. Thou canst not know thy day but through thy brother's night; thou canst not hear thy music but through thy brother's silence. Hast thou pondered these words, "At the evening time there shall be light"? When the joys of thy life have become commonplace, walk in thy neighbour's evening! Dwell in fancy under a sky where these things are absent! Spend an imaginary hour in some garden of withered roses—where thy flowers of every day appear on *no* day! Practise the privation of the pleasures thou deemest stale! Figure thyself without them for a single morning! Fly from thy familiar mountain to spend a moment in another's valley! And his fires shall cleanse thy gold; his clouds shall brighten thy chain; his evening shall bring thee light. Pity shall fill thee with praise; compassion shall teach thee thy comforts; sympathy shall make known to thee thy sunbeams. Thou shalt see thy rainbow through a brother's tears; in the vision of his shadow thou shalt clasp thy joy.

THE EXALTATION OF CHRIST'S SYMBOL

*" The powers of the heavens shall be shaken ; and then shall appear the sign of the Son of Man in heaven."—*MATT. XXIV. 29, 30.*

WHEN is Christ's sign to appear in heaven ? Our Lord says it is when " the powers of the heavens shall be shaken "—" *Then* shall appear the sign of the Son of Man." I take Him to mean that the symbol of Christianity—the Cross— can only appear when the forces of material power have ceased to be objects of adoration. As long as the crushing powers of matter are looked upon with reverence there is no place for the worship of the Cross. As long as the eye of man is riveted on gigantic masses it will have no glance to spare for so unobtrusive a thing as the strength of self-denial. The Cross may be on earth, but it will not appear in heaven—will not be viewed as one of the sublime things. But when in the mind of the beholder the powers of the heavens shall be shaken, when the spectacle of crushing strength shall lose its glory, and the mere height of stature shall cease to be necessarily sublime, then for the first time will be seen the glory of the Son of Man —the glory of stooping, the glory of sacrifice, the glory of self-forgetting love. The shaking need not be an outward one. It is in human *estimation* that the sun shall be darkened and the stars shall fall. The transition wanted is a mental one—a change of opinion. Many an object which our childhood placed in heaven our manhood locates on earth; many a thing which our childhood deemed on earth our manhood claims for heaven. One of these latter is the Cross of Christ. It seems, to-day, a poor thing. In comparison with the might of battalions and the force of artillery, the still small voice of resolute love appears of little weight. But when our estimate of these forces shall be shaken, when materialism shall cease to rule our inward sky, then there shall be a change of government, and the last shall be first. Christ will be glorified. Calvary will be magnified. Pity will be exalted. Mercy will be crowned. Kindness will have a kingdom, tenderness a tiara, sympathy a sceptre, love a laudation—in the day when in the heart the powers of the heavens shall be shaken.

The Exaltation of Christ's Symbol

Hasten, O Lord, that bright and happy morn! I have been seeking in the heavens a purely physical glory. I have been saying, "When I consider the heavens, what is man!" I have seen in the sky other signs than the Cross. I have seen Mars—the symbol of war, Mercury—the symbol of speed, Venus—the symbol of physical beauty, Jupiter—the symbol of the lightning, Neptune—the symbol of the fathomless sea. I have christened no star by the name of the Cross. Why? Because I have thought the Cross unfit for heaven. I have heard no voice say of the *sacrificial* soul, "I go to the heavenly mansions to prepare a place for thee." I have figured war in heaven, I have figured beauty in heaven, I have figured wings of speed in heaven, I have figured fathomless depths in heaven, I have figured lightning flashes of truth in heaven; but I have thought sacrifice a sign of earthly weakness. Reverse the judgment of my heart, O Lord! Show me the strength of the Lamb! Teach me the power of love! Reveal to me the heroism of sacrifice! Inspire me with the greatness of being gentle! Tell me the treasures of the unselfish soul! Put a crown upon the head of the crucified! Proclaim to me that the Christ in the manger is worthy of a star! Then shall I believe that heaven itself holds Thy Cross. Then to me shall the world of spirits be a world of ministration. When I have magnified the work of humanity on earth, I shall discern in the sky the sign of the Son of Man.

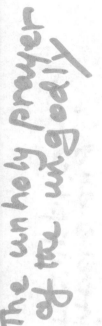

THE UNHOLY PRAYER

" They began to pray Him to depart out of their coasts."
—MARK V. 17.

I THINK this the most unique specimen of prayer which is to be found in the Bible—perhaps the most unique specimen which is to be found anywhere. We are familiar with the prayerless lives of the ungodly. We are familiar with the prayerful lives of the holy. But that prayer should be a weapon of the *un*holy—this is a startling thing. Imagine a congregation assembled in their place of worship. Imagine that in solemn silence every knee is bent and every head bowed in reverent expectation of the preacher's orison. Imagine that through the great stillness the voice that came was this: " O Christ, Thou Son of God, we come this day before Thy Divine Throne to beseech Thee that Thou wouldst be absent from our meeting. We fear Thy presence exceedingly. We find it a drag upon our lives. It forces us to

181

do what we do not wish to do. It makes us submit to painful sacrifices. We feel that we should be richer men, more prosperous men, without Thee. We should have more liberty to cheat and steal, more freedom to appropriate what is not our own. In Thine absence is fulness of joy; in the withdrawal of Thy right hand there are pleasures for evermore; depart from us, O Lord!" What a dramatic thrill of horror would run through the audience! It would be a far greater horror than if the speaker had proclaimed himself an atheist. Discords are always disagreeable; but they are specially so when they are made by a musical instrument. To fight against God by blasphemy is a dreadful thing; but to fight against God by prayer—that seems a thing almost inconceivable. Yet this latter is what was done by the men here spoken of; they breathed discord through a musical instrument. They came to Christ with a real supplication, a sincere supplication, an honest supplication. There was no hypocrisy about it; there lay its sting. It acknowledged Christ, it acknowledged the power of Christ, it acknowledged the character of Christ, it approached Christ on the basis of His character; and with all the forms of devoutness it besought Him to depart.

The Unholy Prayer

My brother, take heed to that for which thou prayest!—there lies the difference between the pious and the impious mind. It is not thy praying that makes thee good—not even thy sincerity in prayer. It is not thy sense of want that makes thee good—not even though expressed in abjectness. It is not thy feeling of dependence that makes thee good—not even thy feeling of dependence on Christ. It is the thing for which thou prayest, the thing for which thou hungerest, the thing for which thou dependest. Every man cries for his grapes of Eshcol; the difference is not in the cry, but in the grapes. It is possible for thee to ask from thy God three manner of things. Thou mayst ask thy neighbour's vineyard—that is bad. Thou mayst ask thine own riches—that is neither bad nor good; it is secular. Or thou mayst ask to be made unselfish—that is holy. It is not thy prayer that thy Father prizes; it is the direction of thy prayer. Dost thou deem thy child a hero because he asks thee for a holiday! Nay, though he sought it sorrowing and with tears. But if he asks thee to let him share his joy with a brother or sister, then thou art exceeding glad, then thou sayest, " Thou art my son; this day have I begotten thee!" So with *thy* Father. He waits till thou criest for a crown—till thou

183

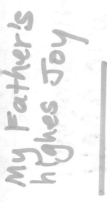

prayest for His presence, longest for His light, sighest for His song, hungerest for His home, faintest for his footfall, callest for His company, tarriest for His tread, seekest for the sign of His coming. That will be thy Father's highest joy.

THE ADVANTAGE OF AFFLICTION

"Moab hath been at ease from his youth, and he hath settled on his lees, and hath not been emptied from vessel to vessel, neither hath he gone into captivity; therefore his taste remaineth in him."—JER. XLVIII. II.

THIS is an extraordinary passage—so extraordinary that if uttered in social life it would be deemed a jest. It is quite a common thing to hear people say, "I pity the poor creature! he is greatly afflicted." But what should we think if we heard one say, "I pity the poor creature! his life has been an unclouded sunshine"? That is what this passage says. It is a striking statement for any man to make, specially striking for a Jew. The son of Israel was by nature a son of the morning. He delighted in prosperity; he rejoiced in the fruits of the land. Yet, it is a scion of this race who utters the words before us—who commiserates the lot of one that has only seen the flowers. I remember some years ago reading a pamphlet of a very exceptional kind, both in subject and ability. It was written by a girl who was a chronic invalid. It was addressed to her fellow-invalids, and it purported to be an appeal for

185

charity towards those who enjoyed unbroken health—an appeal grounded on the statement that such a condition involved want. Now, that is just the burden of Jeremiah's present song. Its subject is, "The disadvantage of unbroken prosperity." He bemoans the fate of one who has never "gone into captivity." He bemoans such a fate on the ground that it gives one a monotonous experience, "His taste remaineth in him." It is not said that the man has a *bad* taste; the whole stress of the evil is laid on the monotony. Jeremiah says that want of suffering produces want of sympathy, and that want of sympathy is want of variety. He feels as sad in beholding a man without sympathy as in beholding a man without sight. As he laments in the one the absence of light, so he laments in the other the absence of shade. For the man without sight he would pray, "Send forth Thy sunshine!" but for the man without sympathy he would cry, "Send forth the shadow of Thy wing!" There is an eye which can only be restored in the night, which needs the *cloud* to make it clear. It must be created at evening-time. It is born of pain—wakened by the wind, wafted by the wave, fostered by the fire, cradled by the cross. That eye is sympathy.

The Advantage of Affliction

Lord, make the clouds my chariots! I "fear" as I "enter into the cloud" as Thy disciples feared upon the mount. It seems to curtail my mountain view, to limit my prospect, to narrow the range of my vision. My ideal of glory has been to build a perpetual tabernacle amid the dazzling light. Teach me that *this* would be the curtailment, this the narrowing! Teach me that I never do get a mountain view of humanity till I have entered into the cloud! I think I understand why it was that Israel had a pillar of cloud by day. She was travelling to meet universal Man, and she could only meet universal Man under a cloud. We are not united by the sunshine; we come not together in the tabernacles on the hill. It is Thy *cloud* that makes us one, O Lord! The rich and the poor have not all the same pleasures; but they have all the same pains. By their pains Thou hast united them. Thou hast linked our brotherhood in the hunger of the heart. Our wings are silver, but our chains are golden. It is by my fetters that I can fly; it is by my sorrows that I can soar; it is by my reverses that I can run; it is by my tears that I can travel; it is by my cross that I can climb into the heart of humanity. Let me magnify my cross, O Lord!

THE EARLIEST CHRISTIAN WONDER

" His disciples marvelled that He talked with a woman."
—JOHN IV. 27.

CHRISTIANITY is the only faith which has found a place for woman. India consigned her to the zenanas; it had no sphere for her amid its castes. It had a sphere for the clergyman, a sphere for the military man, a sphere for the man of commerce; but it never said to the woman, " I go to prepare a place for you." Greece had no mansion for her. Its mansions were for the men of physical prowess; it crowned the sons of battle and the heroes of fame. Judah had no mission for her. It had patriarchs for the family; it had kings for the nation; it had priests for the sanctuary; it had lawyers for the forum; it had masters for the school; it had profits for the individual soul. But it had no province for the woman. It is no wonder that the disciples marvelled at Christianity. It is the earliest marvel at Christianity ever recorded. The little band of Christ's followers had seen the wonders of Jordan, the wonders of Cana, the wonders of the cleansed temple; but I do not read that they marvelled. They *expected* great things of Christ. But they did not expect small things of Christ; and here they found what seemed a small thing. Their wonder was at the Christ *stooping*. They saw the new religion do what no old religion had ever done—reveal itself to those deemed the weak ones of creation. Woman was the creature of emotion, and all emotion was held weak. Desire was esteemed a thing to be crucified before approaching God. The Brahman crucified it by sacrifice; the Buddhist crucified it by will; the Greek crucified it by stoicism; the Jew crucified it by the exclusive contemplation of law. But the woman cried out for a response to her love. It was a voice crying in the wilderness—crying alone. The world laughed and jeered—but the voice cried still. A hundred altars proclaimed, "Ye who worship, extinguish your desires!"—but the voice cried still. Derision could not drown it; contempt could not conquer it; solitude could not silence it—it filled the air with its plaints for replenishment. And then Christ came. He met Woman at the well. She had wandered thither through many lands. She had thirsted by the Ganges, she had been parched in the streets of Athens, she had panted even on the banks of

Jordan; but she was refreshed at last beside Samaria's well.

Lord, Thy disciples will no more marvel at this unique communion. We have learned now that it was the thing religion waited for. We all despised feeling; we thought that the worshipper should empty his heart before offering it to Thee. And so we crushed out emotion and the womanhood that represented it. We put our sister in the zenanas; we treated her as a fallen thing. She had too much of the human and we wanted our religion to "get rid" of humanity. But in the fulness of time *Thou* camest—with a human soul thirsting for human love. Thou camest, and we heard the cry, " Give Me to drink! " Could an impoverished heart answer that cry? Could a heart that had emptied out its feeling respond to Thy prayer for human love? No; only the feminine nature which we had crucified could do that. We had to fall back upon our lost spirit of womanhood. We had to open the zenanas and set our sister free. Nay, we had to make the sister our type for evermore. It is always a *woman's* heart that must now meet Thee at the well. No more with mutilated bodies do we come; we leave that to India. No more with suppressed feelings draw we near; we leave that to Greece. No more with religious fasting do we approach; we leave that to Judah. We bring Thee all our beauty. We give Thee all our gold. We send Thee all our sunshine. We bring our pain to Thy passion, our rapture to Thy rising, our transport to Thy triumph. We trim our lamps to meet Thee; we strew our flowers to greet Thee; we tune our voices to entreat Thee. It is with the gush of a woman's soul we salute Thee at the well.

A NEW ORDER OF NOBILITY

"Behold, what manner of love the Father hath bestowed upon us, that we should be called the sons of God."—
I JOHN III. 1.

A PARAPHRASE familiar to Scottish Churches has thus rendered this passage :—

> "Behold the amazing gift of love
> The Father hath bestowed
> On us, the sinful sons of men,
> To call us sons of God!"

Of course, the sentiment is quite true ; but I do not think it is the sentiment of this verse. I think the amazing feature in the eye of the apostle is not the recognition of *sinful* beings, but the recognition of beings with a particular kind of virtue. I understand him to mean : "What an amazing thing it is that we, of all men, should be called sons of God — we *Christians*, whose qualities are the unobtrusive ones of patience, of meekness, of humility, of peacemaking!" And there was ground for such wonder. The name "sons of God" used to be applied very differently. It was applied to the stars, because they were

192

brilliant and set far above the trammels of earth. It was applied to forms of gigantic strength, because it was deemed greater to be a giant than to be a genius. It was applied to the winners of battles and the conquerors of kingdoms, because the highest victories of man were thought to lie in the physical. But nobody dreamed of applying the name to unrepining invalids, to silent burden-bearers, to patient sufferers, to uncomplaining victims of sacrifice, to those who refrained from reviling and those who worked without reward. It was reserved for Christ to do that. And John says this reveals a new manner of Divine love. It was thought of old that the interest of heaven was centred on earth's mountains—on her places prominent to the eye. I looked at the stars and said, " What is man ! "—I looked at ordinary men and said, " What are these to the making of history ; surely God's providence marks not such humble lives ! " But Christ takes me to a child in the nursery and says, " *That* is the making of history ; on the moulding of *that* depends the fate of nations ! " God's eye is not on the mountains, but on the valleys. It is the *silent* virtues that make the kingdom. Our Father seeth in secret because the great things are in secret. The objects of God's interest are below the sea. His heroes are beneath the cloud. His mighty ones are moving noiselessly. His great events are happening underground; His armies are unseen.

My Father, I should like to read Thy book of life. Thou art now writing Thy book of life— Thy record of human history. When it appears, it will be the final judgment—the ultimate verdict on men and things. It will reverse all previous verdicts; many of the actors whom we put first shall be last and many whom we put last shall be first. The heroes of *Thy* history will be those never heard of before. They will not be the Alexanders, the Cæsars, the Napoleons. They will be some of their unknown ancestors who toiled without groaning, spun without tiring, bore without sinking, endured without dying, and handed down to posterity their soldier-like yet unseen courage. When Thy book is opened I shall learn a strange story. I shall read a new list of the great. No more shall kings appear in the van, no more shall warriors stand in the front. It will be the streams, not the rivers, that will be found to have made glad Thy city. It will be the good mother in the nursery, the frugal father at the plough, the serving sister in the home, the heroic sufferer on the bed, the earnest teacher in the school, the interested master in the office, the prudent companion at the board, the sympathising comforter in the sorrow. It will be Moses not on Sinai but in the desert, Elijah not on Carmel but in the cave, Abraham not in Egypt but on Moriah, John not at Jerusalem but in Patmos, Paul not in his strength but in his blindness. I shall learn in the book of Thy remembrance that it is our moments of obscurity that have made us " sons of God."

THE SPIRITUAL USE OF WORLDLY EXPERIENCE

"Jesus, walking by the sea of Galilee, saw Simon called Peter, and Andrew his brother, casting a net into the sea: for they were fishers. And He saith unto them, Follow me."—MATT. IV. 18, 19.

THIS is not the first call to Peter and Andrew. They had been already called to *conversion*; they are now called to the ministry. Why did not Jesus elect them to the ministry at once? He had made them His disciples when very young men in the wilderness of Judæa. Would not this have been the time to ordain them—to give them a premonition of their coming glory? Why allow the scene of rapture to fade into the light of common day? These young men had at first been caught up to meet their Lord in the air. They had been raised to a height of exaltation; they had gazed upon the beatific vision; they had seen the face of the only-begotten Son of God. Why bring them down again into the coarse life of the world? It would have seemed all right if the world had been the destined sphere of their

196

religious life. But it was not. They were intended
to be preachers, to stand upon the mount and
bless the people. Why, then, not lift them to the
mount in a moment? Why permit them to go
back from the solemn wilderness into the routine
of secular work—into the sphere of the boat-hirer
and the net-mender and the fish-catcher? Was
not the stage between the first and the second call
a waste of time? No, my brother, God's work is
never arrested even where it seems to be. Do
you think it was an accident that after their lofty
flight in the wilderness Peter and Andrew were
sent down to the sea to be fishermen? I tell you
it was a part of the coming call. God does not
want His preachers to be untaught in the present
world. He wants them to know something of
human need and human toil. The fisherman's
life was such a knowledge; it was the satisfaction
of the cry for bread. If the redemption of the soul
did not include the resurrection of the body, our
preachers could be trained in the wilderness. But
it does. Therefore in the training of the preacher,
yea, in the training of the Christian, God has
ordained a drop from the primitive height of
exaltation, a drop into the sea of human trouble
—into the knowledge of human need, human
want, human toil, human care, human doubt and

197

perplexity; the first flight into the air must be followed by a plunge into the sea.

Lord, there have been few moments that have so much disappointed me as my first religious moments. I can remember how on some golden morning I saw the heavens opened and heard the angels sing. I stood upon the mount and looked down, and the things below seemed as grasshoppers. Earth faded into nothingness before me, and I wondered it was a matter of human care. I proposed, like Thy disciples, to build my tabernacle on high—above the sound of the waves, above the friction of the crowd. Suddenly, a cloud came and the glory vanished. I was swept down the hill by an earthly blast—down to the conflict with the storm, down to the waves of the sea. And I cried, " To what purpose is this waste; why bring me from the calm sky to the rough ocean ? " But now, O Lord, I have received Thine answer. It is because Thou desirest the *bridal* of the sea and sky. Thou wouldst not send me on an earthly mission with an unearthly heart. Thou wouldst not send me to Galilee without tasting toil, to Samaria without sympathy for the slighted. Thou wouldst not send me to quell temptations I had never known. Could I dare to rebuke a brother's passion if my own heart were passionless! Could I dare to reprove a sister's temper if my own soul were frigid! Could I blame without knowing the blast! Could I condemn without feeling the conflict! Could I judge the sinner without the sense of his struggle! I thank Thee, O Lord, that Thou didst not send me on my mission in my first enraptured moment. I thank Thee that I was brought down to Jacob's wrestling-ground. I thank Thee that I entered on my mission with a shrunk sinew—a sense of human weakness. I can meet *Thee* in the rapture of an upward flight; but I can only meet my brother in the tossing of an earthly sea.

A NEGLECTED SIDE OF SYMPATHY

"His disciples prayed Him, saying, Master, eat."—
JOHN IV. 31.

THIS I regard as the type of a very peculiar kind of prayer—the prayer expressing solicitude, not for our own welfare, but for the welfare of the Divine Being whom we supplicate. The great mass of petitions addressed to Jesus in the gospels are petitions for our own comfort—for the healing of disease, the recovery of sick friends, the pardon of personal sins, and the like. But this is a prayer of the disciples, not for themselves or their belongings, but for Christ! They are anxious for His outward comfort, for His physical well-being, for the supply of His daily bread. The only prayer in the gospels which I interpret in the same way is the request of the men on the road to Emmaus: "Abide with us, for it is toward evening and the day is far spent." I think, spite of the popular hymn and spite of the undoubted truth of its sentiment, their solicitude was not for themselves, but for Jesus. I think they wished

200

A Neglected Side of Sympathy

Him to find rest after the burden and heat of the day and to avoid the darkening shadows which presaged the coming night. Be this as it may, in the passage before us there never could be a doubt of the interpretation; it is a cry *to* Christ *for* Christ: "Master, eat." Angels ministered to Him in the wilderness; but men ministered to Him in Samaria. The human ministry took the form of prayer—the prayer for His sustenance. I think this prayer must have been very dear to Jesus. Gold is precious because it is rare. This form of petition was also rare, is still rare. The mines of the human heart have seldom yielded such a treasure. Our habitual cry is, "Provide for our human wants, O Lord!" I do not mean that we are purely selfish; we often pray for the satisfaction of needs not individually our own. But it rarely strikes us that these needs are shared by the *Divine.* We often beseech a human friend to take care of himself, to watch his own interests; but we seldom say to the Father, "May *Thy* interests prosper, may *Thy* desires be fulfilled!" We forget that God, too, has a want—the craving of an infinite love. We forget that it is God who says to man, and not man who says to God, "Behold, I stand at the door and knock." We forget that the very infinitude of Divine Love deepens its

201

hunger. There is a need which can only be felt by the Divine heart. A smaller heart can be satisfied; but the boundless ocean of the Father's love has found no bay in which to rest its waters.

Lord, in my prayers let me remember *Thee!* Let me remember that the well of Samaria cannot fill Thy thirst—that the demand of Thy heart exceeds its sources of supply! I pray a hundred times for the satisfaction of my desires; have I ever breathed a wish for the satisfaction of Thine! I have borne in my memory my human brothers who are waiting round the well—those whom I call the objects of charity, those who have been denied the use of the earthly streams. But I have not realised that Thou, too, art waiting at the well. I have not borne in my memory the wants of the Divine. I have not carried in my sympathy the unsatisfied hunger of my God. I have heard the children's cry for bread, but not the Father's cry for fellowship. I have heard the suppliant knocking at my door, but not Thine entreaty knocking at my heart. I have begun to learn that what I call humanitarian sympathy stretches down to the beast of the field, but it has hardly dawned on me that it should also stretch up to heaven. Send me the dawn of that light, O Lord! Help me to frame golden wishes for *Thee!*

A Neglected Side of Sympathy

Make me glad when Thou art glorified, sad when
Thou art stained! Make me jubilant in Thy joy,
transported in Thy triumph, proud when Thou
art praised, blest when Thou art beautified, happy
when Thou art heralded, light-hearted when Thou
art loved, cheered when Thou art cherished, radiant
when Thou hast found Thy day of rest! My
heart will reach its summer by its entrance into
Thy joy.

THE DUTY OF JOYFULNESS

"Let all those that put their trust in Thee rejoice; let them ever shout for joy."—Ps. v. 11.

THESE words were not so much a promise as a command. I understand them to mean, "It is the duty of believers not only to be happy but to reveal their happiness"—not only to "rejoice" but to "*shout* for joy." Gladness is here regarded not merely as a privilege, but as a duty. The idea is that a mournful religion is unfitted to attract. The psalmist wants God to have many votaries. He is annoyed at the fact that men deem the world to have the monopoly of joy. He calls upon believers to counteract that impression. He says: "Ye who love God, do not let the world think that your love has made you miserable. Do not hide your roses. Do not still your laughter. Do not abate your entertainments. Do not lessen the number of your friends. Let not your garments be less gay; drop not a note from your songs. The world may say you are inconsistent; but in truth you alone will be con-

204

sistent. In whom is it consistent to adorn the
body? Is it in those who think it is to perish in
a night? No; gay attire is only justified by the
belief in resurrection. In whom is it consistent
to enjoy the passing hour? Is it in those who
think it will never come back? No; lost joys
should ever make us sad; the half of every
pleasure is the hope that it will endure. In whom
is it consistent to be interested in trifles? Is it in
those who ignore the infinite? No; interest in
trifles should belong to him with whom trifles are
part of the infinite. In whom is it consistent to
bask in human love? Is it in those who hold
that the heart is a bit of mechanism which is set
in motion in the morning and stopped at night?
No; such should *forbid* themselves to love; the
heart is no perfect paradise to him who hears the
message, " Thou shalt surely die." And the
psalmist is right. I am told that the man of God
gets an entrance into a higher than earthly joy.
Doubtless. But I do not see that even earthly
joy is consistent with the absence of God. It
seems to me that the world, like primeval Adam,
has stolen God's apples and put them in its own
vineyard. The tree of life is His as well as the
tree of knowledge. The rivers are His, and the
gold, and the dressing of flowers, and the walk in

the cool of the day. It is written, " Enter ye into the joy of your Lord " ; but the joy of my Lord includes the joys of man.

Lord, many there be that try to show they are Thy people by showing their tears ; but I say with Thy psalmist, " Let all those that put their trust in Thee rejoice." How shall I tempt the world to bathe in Thine infinite sea, if I myself am seen standing in the shallows and shivering with the cold ? Who will believe in the ocean of Thy love if the ships that sail thereon have lowered their flag in sign of mourning ? If men see the inhabitants of Thy heaven arrayed in black robes, will they not justly say, " These are they that *to this hour* are in great tribulation " ? Do not let them wear black robes, O my Father! For all that have come out from the far country, bring forth the bright garments ! Clothe them in white, deck them in jewels, greet them with feasting, surround them with music and dancing ; teach them that, for a converted man, it is good to make merry and be glad ! Turn all eyes that wait on Thee to the rising sun ; may light be sown for the righteous and joy for the upright in heart ! May Thy beauty make us buoyant ; may Thy grace make us gladsome ; may Thy kindness make us kinsmen ; may Thy sympathy make us social ;

The Duty of Joyfulness

may Thy forgiveness make us fellows; may Thy charity make us cheerful; may Thy love make us light-hearted; may the faith in Thy truth make us free from trembling! Let all who trust in Thee unfurl their flag of rejoicing!

THE POWER OF OPTIMISM

"God hath anointed thee with the oil of gladness above thy fellows."—Ps. XLV. 7.

THESE words, as the writer to the Hebrews affirms, were spoken of the coming Messiah. Do they suit the Messiah who has actually come? Anointed with the oil of gladness! Is He not proverbially the man of sorrows? Was not His anointing on the banks of Jordan a call to pain, the inauguration of a sacrificial work foreshadowed in the words, " Behold the Lamb of God " ? Are we to transform our ideal from a man of sorrows into a man of joys—from the image of one who was more marred than the sons of men into the image of one who was distinguished from the sons of men by his gladness? It seems a wondrous revolution of sentiment. But is it? Is there a contradiction between an optimistic mind and a sacrificial mind? I think not. I believe it was the optimism of Jesus that made Him sacrificial. If you ask me what enabled Him to pour out His soul unto death, I can only answer, " It was the glad view He took of humanity." You will find in your experience that the optimistic nature is the sacrificing nature. You spend yourself for a cause in proportion as you have a gladdening prospect of its success. When we speak of Christ as bearing the burdens of His fellow men, we must never forget that it was because He was of all beings the most hopeful for man's glory. He gave His life for the world because none had so rosy a view of the world's possibilities. He was led on to Calvary by the vision of gladness that floated before Him—the vision of a redeemed humanity. No one had sacrificed so much before, because no one had hoped so much before. Christ is the prince of optimists. " While there is life there is hope " is the aphorism of the most sanguine amongst us. Christ goes beyond that ; He has hope even for the dead. There have been men who have healed diseases on the highway ; there have been men even who have sought the living lepers amid the tombs. But Christ bent without despair over the very dead—over the Lazaruses, over the sons of Nain, over the daughters of Jairus. That meant a singularly glad spirit—a spirit so naturally sunlit, so habitually joyous, so prone to the song of the lark, that the spectacle of lifelessness itself could not dispel its morning.

Lord, if I am to do Thy work, inspire me with
Thine optimism! I cannot enter on my ministry
if I am impressed with the utter hopelessness of
the human soul, with the utter worthlessness of
the human body. If I am to watch in the Gethsemane of the sick, I must have a heart not too
heavy. I have read that Thy disciples in that
ward were "sleeping for sorrow." I used to
wonder at the expression; but I see it all now.
They could not *watch* with Thee because they had
no *hope* of Thee—they despaired of Thy cause.
If I am to be kept from sleeping on duty my eyes
must be anointed with the oil of gladness. Anoint
with hope, O Lord, the eyes of all that work for
Thee! Anoint those that tend the couch of pain;
give them the vision, not of death, but of life!
Anoint those who seek to redeem from sin; give
them a vision of the white-robed throng! Anoint
those who visit the homes of the bereaved; give
them the vision of the things that cannot die!
Anoint those that knock at the dwellings of the
poor; give them a vision of the poverty that made
us rich! Anoint those who labour in heathen
lands; give them a vision of the many mansions!
Anoint those who are teachers of the young; give
them a vision of the full-grown man! Anoint
those who are personal sufferers; give them the

vision that they are preparing to be ministering spirits in the kingdom of their Father! Not solemnity but sunshine, not heaviness but happiness, not the weight of reflection but the wing of rapture, is the preparation of those who are called to follow Thee.

THE SEAT OF THE WORLDLY LIFE

"If any man love the world, the love of the Father is not in him."—I JOHN II. 15.

To the mind of St. John the darkest shadow of the human soul is worldliness. Perhaps each of us has a special aversion to some special form of sin. Matthew, Mark and Luke emphasise the horror of blasphemy. Paul lays stress on the danger of unbelief. James is impressed with the evil of idle hands. But John has a special aversion to worldliness. Why? I take the reason to be that he himself had been specially bitten by that form of sin. John had started on the race of life under the impulse of personal ambition. So intense had been that ambition that it had suffused even his religion. He had asked for a front seat in the kingdom of heaven—a seat beside the Lord where he would have a monopoly of the Divine Presence. He had now come to see that this seeming piety was extreme worldliness. And why was it worldliness? Because he was too fond of the society of his brother

212

man ? Exactly the reverse—because he was not fond enough of that society. John's error lay in forgetting the claims of his brother man—in wishing to be alone in his glory. If he had asked that the front seat might be extended so that there might be room for everybody, it would have been all right. But to desire a monopoly of God, to seek an exclusive access to the audience-chamber of the King's Son, this was a breach of brotherhood, and therefore this was worldliness. And that is the reason why John says, "If any man love the world, the love of the Father is not in him." He means that there can be no sense of fatherhood where there is no sense of brotherhood. If worldliness signified anything else than unsociability, there would be no meaning in the statement. If to be unworldly means to be a hermit, why should it indicate the love of God—why should it indicate any love at all ? But if to be unworldly means to be no hermit, if to be unworldly means to be social, if to be unworldly means to have a right hand of fellowship for our brother man, I can understand why it prepares for my love of God. He that loves the brother whom he *hath* seen is ripening for devotion to that common Father whom as yet he hath *not* seen.

Lord, let me not think that the world is a *place* !

The world is me within me

That would lead me to underrate my difficulties. If the world were any particular place, I could easily get rid of it. If it were a theatre or a ball-room or a garden-party, I could soon take the wings of a dove and flee away and be at rest. But the world is none of these things—the world is within me. I can carry it about to any place, and the place to which I carry it immediately *becomes* worldly. Teach me this truth, O Lord! Teach me that, wherever I think of myself alone, that spot is the world! Teach me by the lesson of Thy disciple that I can make my thought of heaven itself a worldly thought! Remind me ever that his most mundane moment was his vision of paradise—his vision of Thy heaven as a place where he was to stand in advance of all men! Impress me with the knowledge that I am not to be driven out of the world, but that I am to drive the world out of *me!* Help me to expel it from my own heart! Reveal to me that to find Thy rest I need no wings of a dove, no flight from the common haunts of men! Crucify the image of my own soul, and I shall hear Thy voice saying, "Go where thou wilt." Drive out the selfish man from the garden of my heart, and there will be no need to remove me from the tree. Create a clean spirit within me, and I shall not fear to live in unclean streets. Bathe *myself* in Jordan's stream, and the wilderness of Judæa and the wedding of Cana will to me be alike unworldly; for alike in the wilderness and at the wedding I shall think of the brotherhood of man.

THE SPECIALLY REPROBATED OLD TESTAMENT SIN

"The covetous renounceth the Lord."—Ps. x. 3 (R.V.).

THIS is the strongest language ever used by the Old Testament of any sin. At first one is surprised that of this particular sin such language should be used. Covetousness seems a trivial fault. It is not a heresy; it is not a blasphemy; it is not a positive hurt to others; it is simply a disease of the individual soul. Yet I do not know of any sin to which the Old Testament attaches such a stigma. "The covetous renounceth the Lord." You will observe, it is not said, "The Lord renounceth the covetous"; the renunciation is on the human side —on the side of the covetous man himself. A greater stigma could not be attached to any sin. Many a heretic *longs* for God; many an agnostic thirsts for God; many a blasphemer speaks in an hour of madness what is not the voice of his sober mind. But to renounce God, to calmly refuse His advances, to repudiate His fellowship, to shut the door deliberately against Him—this is the acme of

Disease of Covetousness: a disease of the individual soul but not trivial—stigma of sin

Renouncing to have anything to do with God

Renunciation of God is on human side

antagonism. And why has covetousness incurred this deadly imputation? It is because the spirit of covetousness is the extreme opposite of the Spirit of God. It is more extreme than atheism. Atheism only fails to *see* a Divine Being; covetousness sees Him quite well and admires not His beauty. That which the covetous man admires is God's opposite. God is love, and the essence of love is giving; covetousness is self, and the essence of self is retaining. God is the converse of avarice. God dispenses charity; avarice gathers gold. God lavishes His treasures; avarice hoards its gains. God lives not to Himself; avarice has no life for another. God seeks out the destitute; avarice hides from meeting the poor. God has many mansions; avarice locks itself in a single room. God scatters sunbeams; avarice picks up pins. God sheds His blood to give life for the needy; avarice sheds the blood of the needy to give life to itself. I do not wonder that a Bible poet once selected as the extreme reverse of godliness, not atheism, but avarice: " Incline my heart unto Thy testimonies and not to covetousness."

My soul, often do I hear thee ask, " Why has my Father put so bad a power within me?" It is not the power that is bad; it is its direction. There is a Divine place for thy covetousness, but it is not the place thou hast chosen for it. Thou hast coveted for thyself; thou wert meant to covet for God. There is a covetousness which is not avarice. The wise men of the East must have passed with their comrades for avaricious men. I marvelled when I saw them so long engaged in gathering earthly gold. I said, " Strange that these eyes which have been trained to search among the stars should have been so attracted by the glitter of things below ! " But by-and-by I saw them carrying their gold to a manger where lay that Infant-Christ for whom the world had no room; and then I knew that they had gathered for Jesus. Seest thou that daughter of Bethany so eager to amass, so anxious to hoard ? She seems a child of avarice. She objects to her sister's absorption in social expenditure—to the many guests at the feast, to the many things provided for them. But wait a little, and the seeming miser will be revealed a spendthrift—a spendthrift for love. She has coveted an alabaster box for Jesus—laden with precious ointment, filled with richest perfume. She wants to lavish it in her love. She knows it will be broken in fragments; but they will be frag-ments of fragrance. She knows it will become a mere memory; but it will be a memory of love— and it is for that she gathers. Be thine her

The Specially Reprobated Old Testament Sin

covetousness, O my soul ! Gather for Jesus ! Grow rich for His poverty ! Seek gold for His service ! Save treasures for His manger ! Practice self-denial for His destitute ! Lay by for His homeless ! Store up for His friendless ! Set apart from Thine own feast for His hungering and thirsting brothers ! Then shall thine be a covetousness which does *not* renounce God.

THE POSTPONED BLESSINGS OF GOD

"My prayer is unto Thee in an acceptable time."—Ps.
LXIX. 13.

PRAYERS are commonly divided into two classes
—those which are conformable to the will of God
and those which are not. The psalmist would
suggest a third class belonging to neither the one
nor the other. He says there may be prayers
which are not conformable to the will of God to-
day, but which will be so to-morrow. There is,
according to him, an acceptable time for the
answering of certain prayers. He does not mean
that there is an acceptable time for *praying*. The
Heavenly Father appreciates prayer whether He
can respond to it or not. The limitation is not to
our petitions, but to God's answers. We often ask
things which are in accordance with God's will,
but for which we are not ready. A young child
asks his father for a knife. Now, that is a possession within the rights of a human being. It is a
possession which one day will be of great use to
the petitioner for the cutting of knots which

220

cannot be untied. But to-day it will cut not the string but the finger—will immolate not the child's difficulties, but the child himself. I am quite sure that the father will for the present refuse the prayer; he will lay up the desired gift in a safe treasury, awaiting the time when its possession will cease to be a danger; it has been asked at a season which is not acceptable. Even so, there are special seasons for the gifts of the Heavenly Father. Many a man asks in April a gift of Divine fruit that will only be ripe in June. Take the case of Paul. Immediately after his conversion he prayed for a mission, " Lord, what wouldst Thou have me to do ? " He was answered by being sent into the solitudes of Arabia. Was the gratification of his prayer denied, then ? No, it was postponed. He had asked at an unacceptable time. He had desired for April the fruits of June. He was not ready for a mission. The light from heaven had overheated him. He needed to be cooled down ere he could deal with the practical wants of men. Accordingly, God prepared for him a place in the wilderness where he could rest and ponder. The mission was coming, but it was coming with the developed years; it was hid in the bosom of the Father till the acceptable time.

My Father, help me to learn that I am heir to

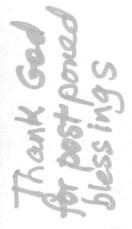

possessions which exceed my present holding! They exceed my present *power* to hold—they are waiting for my summer. Do I ever thank Thee for the blessings which Thou postponest? I am afraid not. I am like the prodigal; I want to get *all at once* the portion that falleth to me; and, where it is not given, I deem it is refused. Teach me, O Lord, the beauty of Thy delayed answers! I have sometimes said in youth, " Lead me in green pastures; make me to lie down by quiet waters." And lo! the road on which I travel has become rough, and the path has grown thorny, and the stillness has been broken by the storm! At such times it has seemed to me as if Thou hadst forgotten to be gracious. Teach me that the form of grace I have asked is not forgotten but postponed! Remind me that youth is not an acceptable time for green pastures and quiet waters! Remind me that Thy best gift to youth is just the rough road and the thorny path and the beating wind! Remind me that at the beginning of life we should not be made to lie down, but to rise up and work vigorously! Remind me that the acceptable time is coming—that I am even now the heir to the reserved blessing! Remind me that Thy day for the green pastures and the quiet waters and the lying down will be the afternoon of my life—when I am weary with the burden and the heat, when I am oppressed with the circuit of the sun! Thy calm is for the midday, O Lord; Thy breeze is for the morning. Let me not ask the calm for the hour Thou hast destined for the breeze; send me Thy fruits in Thine acceptable time!

THE PREPARATION FOR THOSE ON THE RIGHT HAND.

"Then shall the King say unto them on His right hand, Inherit the kingdom prepared for you from the foundation of the world."—MATT. XXV. 34.

"PREPARED for you." Prepared for whom? For the sacrificial souls of humanity—for those of whom Christ said, "I was hungry, and ye gave me meat." The idea evidently is that the future life will be adapted to the spirit of sacrifice. This present world is not adapted to the spirit of sacrifice; it presents barriers to that spirit. There are, I think, two such barriers. For one thing, the world's ideal of heroism is not that of a sacrificial man; it is that of a conquering man. Earth had a laurel wreath for Cæsar; for Christ it had only a crown of thorns. It was prepared for Cæsar; it was not prepared for Christ. But the world has a second and a worse barrier to sacrifice; it is the dimness of our mental vision. We cannot see into the heart of him to whom we minister. We often present a

224

stone when we should give bread. We throw a coin to a beggar who needs a reformatory; we give a tract to a suppliant who needs a coin. We help those whom we should teach to help themselves; we offer work to those who are fit only to be nursed. In these two respects this world is not adapted to the sacrificial soul. But Christ says that in the same two respects the future world *will* be adapted. There, the sacrificial life will be deemed the heroic life. The great men of the New Jerusalem will be the serving men— those who do errands for others; the laurel wreaths will be for Christ and His ministering spirits. And there, the sons of charity will be the sons of *vision*. They will see into the heart of their less favoured brother; they will know exactly what he needs; they will never give the wrong thing. That is what I understand by the words, " Now we see through a glass darkly; then, face to face." Remember where these words occur. In the chapter on charity. Paul is not speaking of our present ignorance of heavenly mysteries; he is speaking of our present ignorance of how to deal with our brother man. He is saying, in effect, that this life is not well adapted for the distribution of charity, and he is anticipating a life where it will be otherwise—a

[margin notes: Ignorance of how to deal with our brother man. The chapter of charity, not well distributed]

life where vision shall be equal to benevolence, where discernment shall move hand in hand with love, where perfect knowledge of our brother's need shall make a perfect provision for our brother's want.

Lord, hasten the happy time when light and love shall meet together; prepare a kingdom for the sacrificial soul! Often here below the problem of human suffering perplexes us; the spirit is willing, but the sight is weak. We know not what is best to do. We cannot tell whether to begin with the strengthening of the soul or the feeding of the body—whether to say "Thy sins be forgiven thee," or "Arise, and walk." Enlighten us, O Lord! We see our brother through a glass darkly; we would behold him face to face. It is for the sake of human charity that we ask Divine light. It is to see the road to helpfulness that we supplicate Thy torch. Not for the sake of speculation do we ask a brighter ray. We seek not to penetrate into Thy deep mysteries. We aspire not to fathom the sea which the angels desire to look into. We crave not to know the secrets that belong to Thyself alone. We pray not to have our personal life lit less by faith and more by sight. Nay, our Father, in all these spheres we would be guided still. But we do

226

THE ENCOURAGEMENT TO CHARITY

"Cast thy bread upon the waters, for thou shalt find it after many days."—ECCLES. XI. I.

THE writer of Ecclesiastes is speaking of the damper which often falls upon our deeds of charity. We say familiarly of many acts of benevolence, "It is just throwing money into the sea." In the days of this writer that saying must have been almost proverbial, for he describes charity by an equivalent expression, "Cast thy bread upon the waters." He admits that benevolence is a throwing of money into the sea—the casting of it out into a sphere of uncertainty. Yet, in spite of that, he bids us throw. He does so on the ground that, though the sea is a sphere of uncertainty, it is not a sphere of hopelessness; many things which are laid on its bosom come back to us again. He tells us that we shall find our bread of charity "after many days." I understand him to mean, "after many castings." I do not think the idea is so much that of time as of

repeated effort. What I take him to say is this:
"You are committing your charities to a very
uncertain medium, and the large majority of them
will probably bear no fruit. But out of a thousand
scattered seeds some few will fructify. Out of the
many to whom your charity may be in vain, there
will be at least two or three to whom it will bring
blessing, and perhaps these two or three may be
more powerful than would have been all the rest
put together. Cast the many seeds for the sake of
the two or three." I agree with the writer of
Ecclesiastes. I hold that charity is always an act
of faith—that it must be bestowed in the absence
of certainty. I hold that it must be tested by its
power to endure many clouds, by its ability to
withstand ninety-nine failures for the sake of the
hundredth case which is to prove a success. I
know a man intimately who has been periodically
solicited for loans of money during a long term
of years, and who has generally acceded to the
request. Of these loans he can only recall one
instance of repayment; but the instance is that of
a boy whom he relieved in an emergency, and who
has lived to be a comfort to his family. The one
success has compensated the many failures. The
bread which has been cast upon the waters has
come back only in fragments; but the fragments

have been so precious that they have justified the
cost.

My soul, let thy charity be the child of thy
faith and hope! Never desist from love through
despair of life! Do not imagine that the value of
a spiritual harvest depends on the amount of the
bread! There were many babes in Bethlehem in
the days of Herod the king, and doubtless much
bread was cast upon the waters for their sustenance. Yet I am told that only one of these
reached manhood; the rest were the victims of
Herod. What then? Was the faith of the
Israelites in vain? No. Who was that one babe
of Bethlehem that reached maturity? It was a
life whose single force was to turn the current of
history, whose single energy was to make all
things new. Say not that thy work is wasted
though thy charity has rescued but one! Hast
thou measured the strength that may lie in one?
There was only one struck by the light at
Damascus; but that one was Paul. There was
only one gained by the mission of Philip; but that
one stood close to royalty. Often in Samaria
thou standest by the well alone, and there seems
no response to the thirst of thy solitary heart. Do
not go away; abandon not yet thy labours! I
see one coming. It is only one; there is no

233

multitude with her. Yet she may be more influential than all that have passed by on the other side. Wait for her, O my soul! Though she is but one, wait for her! Though thou art weary, wait for her! Though the well is deep and the gain seems small, wait for her! Though she comes only by accident and knows not of thy presence, wait for her! Her coming may be the return of the prayers thou hast cast upon the waters.

THE PRAYER OF JAMES AND JOHN

"And James and John come unto Him, saying, Master, we would that Thou shouldest do for us whatsoever we shall desire."—MARK X. 35.

I THINK there is a great difference between the physical and the mental world. In the physical world we ascend from small demands to high ; in the mental we descend from high demands to small. A child begins with simple food and becomes gradually capable of assimilating richer diet. But a beginner in the spiritual life puts out his hand to touch the roof of the universe. His eye rests primarily on the top of the mountain, and it is for that he first aims. In no department is this so conspicuous as in the sphere of prayer. We should expect the history of prayer to be a history of ever-increasing demands—beginning with trifling requests and ending with great requirements. It is the reverse ; it begins with great requirements and it ends with requests which the world would call trifling. We have here before us one of the earliest prayers of Christianity. Two fishermen enter into

235

the presence of Christ to ask a personal boon. We expect that this first flight of prayer will be something modest—the petition for success in their trade, or for comfort in their home, or for support in their duties. To our astonishment, it is the boldest request ever preferred by the lips of mortal man : "We would that Thou shouldest do for us whatsoever we shall desire." I suppose there had come to their ears Herod's promise to Herodias that he would grant her whatever she should ask. They probably said, "If a petty earthly ruler could make such an offer to a member of his family, is it too much to hope that the Ruler of the kingdom of Heaven will do it for His faithful followers?" The word that raises a smile is the word "hope." It never occurred to these men that Herod had not offered a boon at all—that the promise had proved a disaster. For the feature of the prayer is not its presumption ; it is its hurtfulness. Where lies the sting of saying, "Give me whatever I desire"? It lies in the prayer's selfishness. It is impossible that my desire should not at some point cross the desire of my brother. My crops may be crying for rain, and his for sunshine. My heart may be seeking in marriage a human object which he is also seeking. The door by which I would find promotion may be the door at which he himself is knocking. Shall I make my prayer a weapon to strike him down?

Forbid it, Lord; deny the pernicious request! Let my first prayer be, "*Teach* me to pray!" I am more afraid of my desires than of anything else in the world. My deepest fear in prayer, but for Thy love, would be not the refusal, but the granting of it. If I did not know that Thou art love, I should tremble before the gates of my own supplication. I should feel as I do when conflicting armies are on the verge of battle and I expect to hear of slaughter. Shall my petition be the destruction of my neighbour's hope? Shall the flowering of my garden be the withering of his? Shall the bridge by which I cross the river be the mutilated heart of my brother man? Thou, whose name is Love, let it not be! Thou hast made the house of prayer for mutual helpfulness; let me not make it a den of thieves—a place for over-reaching my comrade! Rather let me invert the prayer of these fishermen of Galilee; let me say, "Do unto me whatsoever *Thou* shalt desire!" Let me cast my hopes, not upon my love for myself, but upon Thy love for me! Let me put my interests into *Thy* hands! It is the only confidence I can have that my prayer will be a holy and not a harmful thing. I should like to get my own desires in so far as they coincide with the glory of Thy kingdom —no less, no more. I would not be a favoured one. I would not get the daily bread that is denied to my playmate; it would turn to ashes on my lips. Give Thy crown in common! Light Thy sun on every stream! Impart Thy warmth to a united world! Then only shall I ask the fulfilment of my desire.

THE MORAL INFLUENCE OF HIGH POSITION

"The mountain shall bring peace to the people by righteousness."—Ps. LXXII. 3.

THE mountains have generally brought *war* to the people. This has been increasingly true the further back we go. The unrighteousness of those in high places has brought great misery to those beneath them. The selfish ambition of kings has in times of arbitrary government dragged their unoffending subjects into their own penalties— famine, pestilence, devastation of land, slaughter of kindred, exposure to danger and privation. I think the greatest calamities which have befallen the people of most countries have come from the mountains or high places. Unrighteousness on the mountains has brought dispeace to the people in other spheres than that of war. Take an age of rampant immorality. Analyse its source, and you will find that it has been drafted from the mountains. It has come down to the people as a fashion prevalent in the upper air. It has come

239

down glorified by its previous height. It has lost its association with sin by its association with rank and power; nay, it has been even painted with radiance by the sunbeams on the hill. But the psalmist looks forward to a time when the mountains will have an opposite influence on the people. He says there is a day coming in which the king shall realise that he is a servant of the people, answerable for their moral welfare and bound to maintain their interests. He predicts the advent of an age when individual advantage shall cease to be the motive of earthly sovereigns. He sees in the air the Kingdom of Messiah, the kingdom where the ruler shall be minister to universal need, where the greatest shall be the least, where the wearer of the crown shall be the crucifier of his own passions. And because in the sweet by-and-by he sees beauty on the mountains, he sees it also on the plains and in the valleys. He feels that the tendency of fashion, be it good or bad fashion, is to flow *down*. He feels that the course of virtue, like the course of vice, is not from the provinces to the capital, but from the capital to the provinces. He hails the beautiful feet when they appear upon the mountains, for he knows that from the mountains the tidings most swiftly come, and that the speed of purity is accelerated by the impulse from an upper breeze.

Lord, ever increasingly may the mountains bring peace to the people ! The people take their fashion from the mountains; may the fashion on the mountains be good ! I thank Thee that Thou hast revealed a new ideal of kinghood. I thank Thee that, in Jesus Christ Thy Son, Thou hast taught the humility of being on the height, the responsibility of being regal, the weightedness of wearing a crown. I thank Thee that the sceptre has become associated with stooping, the headship with healing, the royalty with repair of wrong. Place that ideal on the top of the mountain; make each hill where the king sits a " holy hill of Zion " ! Cleanse the mountain air; let there be many lights in the upper chamber ! Put a premium on propriety; make vice disrespectable ! We often say, " I must do in Rome as Rome does"; teach Rome to do well that we may be pure in following her ! I am more afraid of the gilding of sin than of its grossness. If I saw it in itself I should scorn it; but when I see it lighted on the hilltops it assumes a glory. Therefore, O Lord, I beseech Thee to remove it from the hills, to strip it of its false splendour ! Make holy the heights where the great ones dwell! Purify earth's palaces; sanctify earth's sovereigns; stir the conscience of earth's courtiers! Associate kinghood with kindness, power with peacefulness, strength with sympathy, leading with light, government with godliness, empire with earnestness, rank with righteousness, status with stainlessness, brilliance of position with the bearing of human pain! Then shall we look up to the hills for our aid; then shall the mountains bring peace to the people.

HELP FROM THE SUPERNATURAL

"Then came Jesus, the doors being shut, and said, Peace be unto you."—JOHN xx. 26.

IT is not always that Christ comes into the soul when the doors of the world are shut. To the apostles themselves He had originally come through the world's *open* doors. He had reached them in the course of their daily labour. He had met Peter by the sea, Matthew at the receipt of custom, Thomas in the exercise of his intellect. Most of His followers had been found in a pleasant environment—Nathanael under a tree, Zacchæus on the top of a tree, Martha and Mary and Lazarus in the family circle, the shepherds in the watching of their flocks, the astronomers in the observing of a star, the men of Cana in the feast of nuptial joy. But there are times when Christ comes, not through the open, but through the shut, doors of life—when no flowers clothe the fig-tree, when the flock is cut off from the

243   Q 2

fold, when the board of Bethany is spread no more, when the treasures brought from the East are exhausted, when the vine has denied her fruit to Cana and the nuptial joy is silent. Even at such a time of closed doors the peace of Christ has often entered the soul. You have heard one say at times, " I cannot get up my spirits; I know not how it is; every door is open to me, yet life feels flat and poor." But there is another and an exactly contrary experience. There are seasons when you hear one say, " I cannot let *down* my spirits; I know not what is keeping me up; all the doors of life are shut, yet I cease not from my song." It is rather a singing than a soaring, rather a keeping-up than a flying on the wing, rather a peace than a transport. I do not at such moments believe the doors to be open when they are shut; I am simply conscious of a warm fire inside, which will not let me feel desolate. Whence the fire comes, I cannot tell. Eye hath not seen its kindling; ear hath not heard its crackling; heart hath not conceived the fuel by which it flames. It warms without wood, it comforts without coal, it heats without hands, it subsists without sustenance, it renews without replenishing, it lasts without human labour; it is the peace of God.

Help from the Supernatural

O Thou who hast brought a resurrection life into a world with shut doors, I too, when my doors are shut, may be reached by Thee. There are days when all my avenues are closed. There is no entrance from the front—the future is cloudy. There is no entrance from the back—the retrospect is sombre. There is no entrance from the side—the things of life are adverse. There is no entrance from the roof—like the patriarch Job I have lost sight of the open heaven. Men look and say, "A doomed house, a sealed house, a house where the inmate must die." Yet, in such a house Thy resurrection life can dwell. Thou canst enter without doors. Thy peace can tread where there is no pathway; Thy rest can travel where there is no road. There is a light which surprises—it shineth in darkness. Thou hast birds that sing where there is no summer; Thou hast flowers that bloom where there is no sun; Thou hast faces that smile where there is no outward fortune. Send me, O Lord, Thy supernatural joy—Thy grandly unreasonable rest! Dawn in my darkness! Glitter in my gloom! Fan into flame my emberless fireplace! Send me steadfastness in the storm! Lend me nerve in the night! Give me bravery in the loss of battle! Cheer me in the chill! Warm me in the winter! Lighten me spite of my load! Prepare for me a feast in the presence of my foes! Let the lamb lie down with the lion—let the calm subsist amid the world's roar! Then shall I know that Thy peace is not born of earthly things.

CHRIST'S NATIONAL JUDGMENT

"When the Son of Man shall come in His glory, then shall He sit upon the throne of His glory ; and before Him shall be gathered all nations ; and He shall separate them."—MATT. XXV. 31, 32.

I UNDERSTAND the idea to be, " There is a time coming in which the worth of a nation will be measured by its conformity to the standard of the Son of Man."   Put into modern language, the prophecy is this, " The nations at the right hand of power will be the nations animated by the love of humanity."   Wherever the Son of Man has come in His glory—wherever the welfare of humanity is the paramount thing, the humanised nations are the powerful nations.   Before men recognised the glory of a human soul the power of a nation lay in something material.   The great kingdoms were the kingdoms of physical force, of crushing strength, of warlike prowess ; their symbol was the lion and the panther.   But when an individual man was enthroned in the heart of the world, when the most attractive object in the

universe became a sacrificial human soul, then the
first was made last and the last first. The kingdoms of physical force faded and the kingdoms of
moral force advanced. When the sign of the Son
of Man appeared in heaven, those nations came to
the front that recognised the rights of man. The
lands of liberality became the lands of light. The
empires of intolerance receded; they passed to the
left of the throne. Despotism withdrew into the
desert. Tyranny went back with the tide.
Slavery retreated to the silence. Monopoly was
hidden in the mist. The free nations stood fore-
most. Europe outstripped Asia; America outran
Africa; the West left the East behind. Culture
suppressed cruelty. Charity broke man's chain.
Love restrained law. Pity softened power.
Service eclipsed sovereignty. Kindness outshone
kinghood. Meekness became more potent than
majesty. The roaring of the lion was drowned in
the pleading of the lamb.

Lord, may Thy kingdom come! May it come
not in the clouds of heaven, but in the cloudless-
ness of earth! We thank Thee that already we
hear it on its way. We thank Thee that the
wheels of Thy chariot draw nearer. We thank
Thee that the nations at the right hand of power
are the humanitarian nations. We thank Thee

that the empires which oppressed the rights of man have taken the left side and sunk into the shade. Nearer and nearer, O Lord, may that kingdom come—the kingdom of humanity! Swifter and swifter may that chariot roll—the chariot of the Son of Man! More and more may the eyes of the nations rest on the glory of a human soul! May ever deeper grow their enthusiasm for the work of Jesus—their desire to serve Him, their eagerness to follow Him! May they feel that a kingdom is only great when it is sprinkled by His Spirit! May they learn that from Him come all the qualities of their soldiers—the chivalry, the courage, the endurance! May they learn that from Him come all the qualities of their statesmen—the wisdom, the prudence, the foresight! May they learn that from Him come all the qualities of their teachers—the patience, the clearness, the tenderness! To Him may they trace their happy homes, their domestic endearments, their lamps of family love! To Him may they ascribe their boast of brotherhood, their social sympathy, their mutual membership! To him may they dedicate their chalice of charity, their cup of kindness, their ministry to man! To him may they attribute the survival of their sick, the healing of their helpless, the life of their languid, the fire of their feeble, the wealth of their weak, the song of their sorrowful, the bravery of their baffled, the hopefulness of their heavy-laden! May they find the secret of their right-hand place in this, that he who sits upon their throne is the Son of Man!

INDIVIDUAL IMMORTALITY

"To every seed its own body."—I COR. xv. 38.

PAUL is speaking of the soul in the future state. It is the boldest assertion of individualism I have met with in all literature. What is it that makes you and me individuals? It is not the fact that each of us has a body, but that each of us has "his *own* body"—a body different from others. It is our difference that makes us individuals. I heard an eminent theologian once say that, in his opinion, when we get to heaven we shall all think the same thing at the same time. This was *his* notion of reconciling the individual with the universal. I should call it the *killing* of the individual by the universal. In such a state we might have communion with God, but we should never have communion with one another. What is it that makes the communion between any two souls? It is their mutual exchange of ideas. To think the same thing at the same time is *not* to exchange ideas. You may set your clocks so as to strike the same hour at precisely the same moment. That is exactly what such a heaven

251

would be. If the living timepieces in the many mansions of our Father's house are to strike the hours uniformly and simultaneously, we shall all be harmonious, but we shall cease to be individuals. What constitutes me a separate man is just the fact that the clocks do *not* sound uniformly nor simultaneously. Our separateness is not our sameness, but our communion. Communion demands difference—individuality. If you and I meet on the road some day and both exclaim in a breath, "It is very fine weather," what have we given to each other? Nothing; we have simply *expressed* ourselves, uttered our united opinion. There is a great deal too much of this in the present world—union without communion. God says He will make it different yonder—a man will keep his own. Heaven will restore the individuality which earth has broken; we shall all be self-revealing in the sweet by-and-by.

Lord, I have heard men say that death will rob me of my personal life. But Thou hast told me it is this world that robs me and that death will restore it. Here, I have not my own body; I have the body of the community; I am wound up to speak the same words that the world speaks. But yonder, I shall be an individual soul—unconventional, spontaneous, free. I shall have my

Our separateness is not our Sameness but our Communion— Communion demands difference—individuality

Avoid union without Communion

own body—not another's. I shall not merely accompany the stroke of a neighbouring timepiece; my *own* hour will have come—the hour for self-revealing. The fashion of this world is conformity; but the fashion of Thy world will be difference. *Thy* conformity is not a united hour-stroke but a united song. It takes many different notes to make a song; to be a member of Thy choir invisible I must sing my own part. Let me practise that part now, O Lord! Let me find, on earth, my place in the choir above! Let me not be distressed though I strike not the key of another! If I have failed to walk upon Peter's sea, let me not be discouraged thereby!—Thy part for me may be the inland lake. If I have failed to flash Elijah's fire, let me not be downcast thereby!—Thy part for me may be the still small voice. If I have failed to climb the Mount with Moses, let me not be ashamed thereby!—Thy part for me may be the modest vale. I ask not the note of my brother; I ask the power to blend with it. May the lark keep its morn and the nightingale its eve! May the wise men meet their star and the shepherds their flock! May Cana yield Thee her wine, and Bethany her domestic joy, and Nain her ministry to tears! The varied sounds will make one harmony in the song of Thy redeemed.

Effect of cure
from effect of
sin's expulsion

THE EFFECT OF SIN'S EXPULSION

"When she was come to her house, she found the devil gone out, and her daughter laid upon the bed."—MARK VII. 30.

THE immediate effect of cure is not a sense of exhilaration. This is true even of physical illness; the patient is most apt to feel his weakness in the hours of convalescence. But it is supremely true in the spiritual world. This maiden had been what we should now call regenerated; an evil spirit had been cast out of her. Yet the immediate effect is not encouraging. Instead of being elevated she is prostrated; she is found lying on a bed. She had lost her old energy. That energy had come from delusive desires; but it had probably made her charming. She had found that she had been chasing a shadow; but, during the chase, she had been brilliant. To find that it had been a shadow was gain; but it was gain that involved loss—not permanently indeed, but for to-day and to-morrow. It took away the zest from life; it dimmed for a time the sparkle of the eye; it substituted the heavy step for the wings of an eagle. A disillusioned soul is like a weaned

254

child. When a young man first abandons the wine-cup he probably for a time abandons something more. He may lose his sparkle, his humour, his brilliancy. He may lack the genial jest, the ready repartee, the mirth that made others merry. His comrades may miss in him the laugh that brought light and the charm that gave cheer and the buoyancy that for a night banished care. He has had to pay for his freedom, and it is no wonder if for an hour he is impoverished. It is a dreary season between Egypt and Canaan. It is well called a desert. Our treasures are often wrapped up in our trespasses so that to part with the latter is to part with the former. The resurrection from sin reveals at first but an empty tomb where the spices of life are useless and there is nothing worthy to be embalmed.

And yet, my Father, such is not the rest Thou hast in store for me. Thou hast not lifted me out of the passions of sin that I may enter into a life of passionlessness. I may be exhausted for a day, I may be prostrated for a night upon my bed. Yet my goal is not a couch, but a crown. There is coming to me a new passion, a fresh energy, a second youth. Hast Thou not said that the joyous things of this world are but shadows of things to come? Yes, my Father, and therefore

255

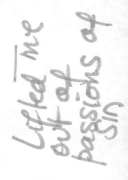

Thoughts for Life's Journey

I shall get back the equivalents of all that I have lost. Beyond these forty days of the wilderness there glimmers the light of a second Cana where the water once more shall be turned into wine. Thy latest word to every soul is this: "Arise, take up thy bed and walk!" Mine will be again the sense of morning, the glad look-out, the prospect of a promised land. Mine will be again the impulse of the young, the heat of expectancy, the blood made rapid by hope. Mine will be again the disbelief in limitations, the confidence in destiny, the faith that mountains will be removed. Mine will be again the poet's dream—the belief that somewhere there is a city paved with gold. Mine will be again the communion of brotherhood —joined by the cup that quickens yet inebriates not, that dwarfs the care without making oblivious of the joy. Mine will be again the forgetfulness of earth's decay—the trust that love will last, the hope that charity will be changeless, the sense that pity will be permanent, the faith that affection will abide, the instinct that sacrifice will survive, the assurance that between man and man devotion will not die. The fruits of Thy new world will give back the vintage of the old; he who begins upon the bed will culminate on the wing.

THE ATTRACTION OF THE GREEK MIND TO JESUS

"Certain Greeks came therefore to Philip, saying, Sir, we would see Jesus."—JOHN XII. 21.

IT is no wonder that the Greeks desired to see Jesus. The ideal of the Greek was always the man whose character avoided extremes. What he praised above everything else was the middle way—the golden mean. He had four favourite virtues—prudence, the middle line between anxiety and recklessness; temperance, the middle line between excess and abstinence; fortitude, the middle line between daring and cowardice; and justice, the middle line between good nature and severity. Now, I think that from the human side Jesus was essentially the man of the golden mean. He is that which the Greek waited for, but which, in his own nation, he never perfectly found—the man who had in him a little of everything. The proof is, the diversity of those who followed Jesus. I say, the diversity—not the number. A hundred followers of Jesus are more proof of His power than are a million followers proof of the power of Buddha. The men of Buddha are all of one type—they are of the East Eastern. But the men and women of Jesus are of many moulds. Why is one of His disciples so unlike another? It is because the Master never exhausts Himself in one type; He has a little bit of all lives in Him. He is the mediator—the middle man; He joins opposite shores. Peter is there with his impulse, and John with his calmness. Nathanael is there with his faith, and Nicodemus with his reasoning. Martha is there with her work, and Mary with her mysticism. Paul is there with his poetry, and James with his prose. He has songs of Bethlehem for the child, and Jordan visions for the youth, and heights of Hermon for the man. Joy can meet Him at Cana; depression can find Him at Gethsemane. He can join in the prattle by the fireside, and talk with the learned in the law. He can speak with the peasant on the highway, and discourse with the ruler of the synagogue. He can support the social order, and yet ward from its destructive stroke the victim that has wandered from the way. Oh, I do not wonder that the Greeks sought Jesus! He was the man for whom they were specially made—the man all-round. They had dreamed of Him in the night, and had been gladdened by their dream; and in the waking world they found the original—standing in the dawn.

Lord, to us as to the Greeks, Thou art the fulfilment of a dream. Ere ever we had seen Thee Thou wert the desire of our hearts. We, like the Greeks, have all wanted a mediator—a middle-man—a man who had in him something of all men. Humanity could never have been attracted by any *one* quality, however grand. We could not tell the invalid to take comfort from the strength of Samson: that was the very thing which made her despair; she wanted one that had tasted weakness too. We could not tell gentle Ruth to imitate warlike Deborah: that would have been to kill her gentleness; she wanted one that could give her power through peace. But when *Thou* camest, there came a universal man, an intermediate man, a man with a touch for all. Within Thy heart slept all contraries in concord. The lion was there and the lamb, the thunder and the still small voice. The strength of Samson was there; but it was perfected in weakness. The fire of Elijah was there; but it was kindled by tender love. The activity of Martha was there; but it was winged by hours of rest. In Thy one hand a telescope swept the stars; in the other a microscope searched the dust. Thy voice came from the mountain; but its precepts were made for the valley. All extremes met in Thee—joy and sacrifice, love of the sinner and loathing of the sin, power and gentleness, storm and peace, rebuke and pity, passion and placidness, depth and simplicity, ocean and stream. O Thou mediating man that had a share in all, let me find my part in *Thee*!

THE PLACE FOR SUCCESSFUL INQUIRY

"When He was entered into the house from the people, His disciples asked Him concerning the parable."—MARK VII. 17.

THERE are times for religious inquiry. Strange to say, they are the times not of mental tossing, but of mental rest. It was when Jesus was entered into His own house and when the door was shut against the noise of the multitude, that His disciples began to question Him. The reverse view is the popular one. The prevalent notion is that the spirit of inquiry is fostered by the noise of antagonism, that the real place for it is *outside* the house of Jesus. That is a grand mistake. The psalmist of Israel knew better; he expressed the wish to dwell in God's house and see His beauty in order that he might "inquire." He felt that no man is qualified to get an answer if he is in a state of tumult. And is he not right? Is it not a matter of daily experience that the mind which inquires successfully must be a mind at rest? "Be still, and know!" cries the Divine oracle. You will never come to know by being violent. If you want to hear an answer to your questioning, you must come inside the house and escape the clamour of the multitude. Neither you nor Elijah can hear God when the heart is convulsed by thunder and earthquake and fire. Many a message to the soul has been lost by the soul's own storm. The world did not hear the coming of its Christ. Why? Because the world's heart was in great unrest. Mary did not recognise the form of the risen Lord. Why? Because Mary's soul was in deep despair. Martha did not catch the sweet words at Bethany. Why? Because Martha's spirit was careful and troubled about many things. Our crowns of glory often need to be "laid up" for us. They are lying at our feet, and we do not lift them. We believe them to be stones on the causeway. We miss the glitter of their gems; we see not the sparkle of their gold. We are too distraught to recognise them—too close to the clamour, too near to the multitude. We must get inside if we would find our crown; we must enter the house with Jesus. We must get the calm mind, the placid conscience, the rested heart, the bending will, the quiet patience, the tranquil faith, the underlying peace, the optimistic love; then shall we hear the answer to the questioning of our souls.

The Place for Successful Inquiry

Bring me into Thy house, O Lord, that goodness and mercy may follow me! Goodness and mercy have been with me all the days of my life; but when they first come I do not see them; they have to "follow me." It is only when I have entered Thy house that I really recognise them. It is only in the peace of Thy home, in the calm of my spirit, that I know how great have been my benefits. I thought I was speaking to the gardener; when I entered Thy house I found that it was Jesus. I thought I was walking to Emmaus with a stranger—mine eyes were blinded with grief; when I entered Thy house I found it was the risen Lord. I thought I was clothing a child in a manger; when I entered Thy house I found I had been robing the Son of Man. I thought I was giving drink to a suppliant at the well of Samaria; when I entered Thy house I found that I had met the *answerer* of prayer. I thought that Calvary had crucified the Christ; when I entered Thy house I saw that it had crowned Him. I thought that the box of ointment was wasted when it was broken; when I entered Thy house every corner was filled with its fragrance. I have seen the mercies of the midday only by the cool of evening; I have learned the world's beauty in the quiet of Thy home.

THE TRUE VICTORY OVER SORROW

"The land whereon thou liest, to thee will I give it."—
GEN. XXVIII. 13.

THE words are spoken to the prostrate Jacob
on his stone pillow at Bethel, and the promise is
the strangest ever conceived. "I will give thee
the land whereon thou liest—the scene of thy
humiliation, the place of thy prostration, the spot
where thou art now a starving vagrant." There
is something startling here. It is no uncommon
thing for a man in the hour of his adversity to
have a vision of better fortune; I do not wonder
that even upon his pillow of stone Jacob should
have had a dream of coming glory. But this is
more than a dream of coming glory. It is a
dream which says, "There is a time coming in
which your glory shall consist in the very thing
which now constitutes your pain." Nothing could
be more sad to Jacob than the ground on which
he was lying. It was the hour of his poverty.
It was the season of his night. It was the seeming
absence of his God. His deepest thought at the

264

time was that God had forgotten him. His one cry of subsequent surprise is this, "The Lord was in this place, and I knew it not!" It was the only moment in his life when he felt deserted by Heaven, when he was disposed to say, "My way is hid from the Lord." And yet the dream declares that this rejected moment is to be the scene of his glory—"The land whereon thou liest will I give thee, the place of thy prostration will be thy paradise." There is no promise in the world so sweet to a distressed soul as this. The promise of deliverance is dear, but it is not the dearest. If I have been prostrated on an earthly bed, it is something to know that one day I shall get Easter wings and fly away. Yet even in my upward flight should I not feel that I had wasted time? Should I not feel that while I lay upon my pillow of stone I had lost a day's work in the vineyard, that the world was moving on and had left me a march behind? But when the voice says, "The ground whereon thou liest shall be thy glory," this indeed is victory. It is not mere Easter morning; it is the Easter of Calvary. It is not the resurrection into shining garments; it is the resurrection of the man with his grave-clothes. It is not the forgetting of the rents in the old robe by putting on a heavenly vesture; it

265

is the finding of a place of beauty for the print of the former nails. The day of my trial has been the dawn of my triumph.

My soul, reject not the place of thy prostration! It has ever been thy robing-room for royalty. Ask the great ones of the past what has been the spot of their prosperity; they will say, "It was the cold ground on which I once was lying." Ask Abraham; he will point you to the sacrifice of Moriah. Ask Joseph; he will direct you to his dungeon. Ask Moses; he will date his fortune from his danger in the Nile. Ask Ruth; she will bid you build her monument in the field of her toil. Ask David; he will tell you that his songs came from the night. Ask Job; he will remind you that God answered him out of the whirlwind. Ask Peter; he will extol his submersion in the sea. Ask John; he will give the palm to Patmos. Ask Paul; he will attribute his inspiration to the light which struck him blind. Ask one more—the Son of Man. Ask Him whence has come His rule over the world. He will answer, "From the cold ground on which I was lying—the Gethsemane ground; I received My sceptre there." Thou too, my soul, shalt be garlanded by Gethsemane. The cup thou fain wouldst pass from thee will be thy coronet in the sweet by-and-by.

The True Victory Over Sorrow

The hour of thy loneliness will crown thee. The day of thy depression will regale thee. It is thy *desert* that will break forth into singing; it is the trees of thy silent *forest* that will clap their hands. The last things will be first in the sweet by-and-by. The thorns will be roses; the vales will be hills; the crooks will be straight lines; the ruts will be level; the mist will be heat; the shadows will be shining; the losses will be promotions; the tears will be tracks of gold. The voice of God to thine evening will be this, " Thy treasure is hid in the ground where thou wert lying."

CHRIST'S SYMPATHY WITH PAUSES IN LABOUR

" They passed through Galilee ; and He would not that any man should know it."—MARK IX. 30.

I THINK this passage reveals a singular experience on the part of the Son of Man. You must carefully distinguish it from those passages in which He wishes to conceal His Messiahship. Here it is not His Messiahship that He wants to hide, but Himself; He desires no one to be told that He is passing through Galilee. It is quite a common thing for kings and great personages to travel incognito. Their motive in so doing is to avoid publicity. They are oppressed by the weight of their own personality. They are weary of being objects of the world's wonder. They are tired of being surrounded by crowds, whose only purpose is to gaze. If they were *helping* these crowds, they would feel otherwise; but to stand as a target for curiosity is to bear the fatigue of the treadmill—to bear a fatigue which accomplishes no work and achieves nothing for the world. Now, in one of His journeys, Jesus had this desire to be hid, to be saved from any weariness which was not part of the redemption of mankind. I am glad that the evangelist has recorded this seemingly commonplace experience. I am glad he has recorded it, just because it is commonplace. I like to think of every experience of my life as having found a counterpart in Christ. It is more easy to find these counterparts in proportion as we ascend to great things. The bankrupt may find it in His impoverishment, the physical sufferer in His pain, the bereaved in His Bethany, the deserted in His betrayal, the hungry in His wilderness, the thirsting in His cross, the homeless in His having not where to lay His head, the sleepless in His midnight tossing on the waves. But there are little moments less grave than these for which yet we fain would find a counterpart, times when we are not miserable, but just weary of the burden and the heat, and longing for a holiday of change. Is it not something to know that these commonplace moments, these unromantic moments, these moments which seem the most unheroic in the life of man, have found a kindred spot in the sympathy of Him who, in the days of His flesh, bore the frailty of our frame?

269

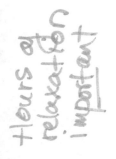

Thoughts for Life's Journey

Lord, I thank Thee for this sidelight on Thy sympathy. It gives a solemnity to the things I thought least solemn—my hours of relaxation. I have always associated Thy sympathy with my hours of toil. I have had no difficulty in praying for Thy presence in the sphere of duty, in the discharge of my work for my brother man. But it never occurred to me to say, " Be with me in my desire for a holiday, in my search for relaxation of the business cord." At such times I seemed to myself a trifler, a poor creature, a revealer of the weak side of human nature. I shall not think so any more. In Thy desire to pass through Galilee unknown to the crowd, I shall see henceforth the sanctifying of what I call my hour of idleness. For, let me not forget, O Lord, that there are holy thoughts which can only come through a holiday. Many a ship of beauty passes unseen, in the night which my own anxiety has made. Many a rose of comfort has been covered unwittingly by my own working hand. Many a song of immortal hope has been curtained from my ear by the roar of the loom and factory. Many an angel's wing has been hid from my view by the smoke and dust of duty's battle. I thank Thee that Thou hast sympathy with my strain of tension. I bless Thee that I can think of my relaxation as Thy rest. I praise Thee that in the unbending of my bow I can see the breaking of Thy bread. I laud Thee that I can cease to deem my hour of freedom an hour of frivolity. The secrecy of Thy road through Galilee has made it religious to repose.

(3) Sources of comfort in sorrow
The future, the present, the
Past.

THE COMFORTING SPOT IN MEMORY

"I call to remembrance my song in the night."—Ps. LXXVII. 6.

THERE are three sources of comfort in the hour
of sorrow—the future, the present, and the past.
The comfort of the future is anticipation—the
looking forward to better things.   The comfort of
the present is strength—the support of an invisible
hand.   The comfort of the past is memory—a
recalling of the experience of former days.   The
psalmist is here speaking of the last of these.   It
is interesting to observe where he thinks the special
comfort of memory to lie.   He does not seek it
where I should expect him to seek it.   I should
expect him to recall life's unclouded days, to bring
up to remembrance whatever moments he has had
of unqualified joy.   He does not. On the contrary,
he seeks the proof of Divine help by going back
not to his bright, but to his chequered, hours, "I
call to remembrance my song in the night."   What
he says is this, "Your best comfort from memory
is not the recalling of days when you had no cloud,

272

but the recalling of days when you had mingled cloud and sunshine—the memory that the song could exist in the sorrow." Why is the memory of these chequered moments the psalmist's best comfort in tribulation? It is because they reveal a phase of God's presence which is not revealed by the remembrance of unqualified joy. If I am in grief, I would rather remember that God once rescued me than that He once regaled me. If I am lying among the thorns, it is no great solace to know that yesterday God laid me among the flowers; if that were all, it might mean that He can only love the beautiful. But if I can remember how, when yesterday I lay among the thorns, He planted flowers beside me—if I can remember that His song came to me at the very moment when the pulse of life beat low, then indeed I get from retrospect a unique revelation—God's presence in calamity. Every Jew believed in His presence *outside* calamity. Every son of Israel recognised His favour in man's song and His absence in man's night. But the psalmist wants more. He wants to feel that the night may itself have a song, that the cloud may itself have a bow, that the thorn may itself be environed by a rose. God's glory to him is His presence in the gloom.

Lord, I am grateful for the memory of green

pastures and quiet waters; but in the hour of sorrow my comfort is *another* remembrance—Thy rod in the path that is rugged, Thy staff in the waters that are *not* still. Methinks when I look back I never see Thee so clearly as in Thy coming with clouds; Thou art brightest against a dark ground. I do not say that I have never failed to find an *explanation*; but I have never failed to find a rod and a staff. The comfort of memory is not that I have traced my sorrows, but that I have sustained my sorrows. In looking back I do not always see my emergence from the shadow; but I can always see that there was support in the shadow. How do I know that Thy rod and Thy staff were with me? Simply because I did not die. My retrospective marvel is just that I have got through. I do not understand *how* I have got through. I only know that my own strength could not have done it, that my own unaided steps could not have done it. Something must have kept me up. Something must have helped me to walk through the valley of the shadow. It was Thy rod and Thy staff, O Lord. It is this which makes the dearest spot in my memory the valley of the shadow itself—not the pastures green, not the still waters. In the pastures green Thou wert with me in my greatness; by the still waters Thou wert with me in my strength. But in the valley of the shadow Thou wert with me in my weakness. It was a meeting of extremes. Thy mercy came to my meanness; Thy power came to my poverty; Thy hand came to my heaviness; Thy bracing came to my burden; Thy song came to my sigh; Thy life came to my lowliness; Thy radiance came to my rags; Thy glory came to my grief. The most comforting spot to me will always be the valley where I heard Thy song.

THE FIRST SYMPTOM OF CONVERSION

"And Saul arose from the earth; and when his eyes were opened, he saw no man."—ACTS IX. 8.

THE immediate effect of Saul's illumination was a sense of darkness. It seems a wild paradox. But in the spiritual world it is the experience of every enlightened man. It is true even of secular development. The first manifestation of every mental light is a sense of mystery. It does not exist in the child. Children have not a feeling of mental blindness. They are not conscious of difficulty, are not overawed by the things around them. They do not experience the need of picking their steps or walking warily. They appear, to themselves, to see everything plainly. The reason is that the light has not come and that therefore the sense of blindness has not come. The first effect of larger light will be decreasing confidence. There will come by-and-by a stage called wonder. What is wonder? I should define it to be the soul's sense of its inability to see. We begin to marvel at a thing when we find that we do not see

276

through it; and what enables us to have the experience is an increase of mental light. The feeling of incompetency in the inward eye is created by the new flash of intelligence. So is it in the religious life. When God illuminates a soul the new power of vision manifests itself as mist. When Saul of Tarsus gets his enlightenment he experiences for the first time an inability to walk alone. The immediate gift of God to him is a sense of insufficiency. He had not felt it yesterday; his prevalent feeling yesterday was a sense of individual power. But to-day the light has come and the self-sufficiency has died. He is unable to find his way along the same road on which yesterday he strutted with the most confident and fearless step. It is the same road, the same company, the same outward man; what makes the difference? An inward something—light. It is that which makes him feel the sense of impotence; it is that which makes him cry, "O wretched man that I am!" If a grown man got his sight for the first time, he would for the first time feel blind. He would cease to find his way in the old paths; he would need to be led about awhile. So with God's illumination. It makes old things new, and therefore I do not recognise them; it causes me to cry out for the leading of my Father.

Lord, Thou hast arrested me on my Damascus journey; Thou hast transformed self-consciousness into humility. I set out on the road with boundless belief in myself; I felt no obstacle, I experienced no difficulty. Suddenly, at a turning of the way my soul grew paralysed. The confidence faded. The world no longer stretched before me as a pleasure-ground. There came a mist over the scene, and I could not find my way. It all happened in the meeting with one man—a man from Nazareth. Before I met Him, my pride of self was unbounded; I said in my heart, "I shall carve my own destiny." But one glance at the man of Nazareth laid me low. My fancied glory became ashes; my imagined strength became weakness; I beat upon my breast and cried, "Unclean!" Shall I repine because I met that man! Shall I weep because a flash of light at a street corner threw all my greatness into shade! No, my Father, for the shade is the reflex of the sheen. It is because I have seen Thy beauty that humanity has grown dim. It is enlargement that has made me humble. I have gazed for a moment on a perfect ideal, and its brightness has eclipsed my candle. It is not night, but day, that blinds me to my own possessions. It is light that makes me loathe myself. It is sunshine that reveals my soiledness. It is dawn that tells me of my darkness. It is morning that discloses my mean attire. It is the glow that spots my garments. It is the clearness that numbers my clouds. O God, my God, I only lose my way when I am lit by Thee!

REJUVENESCENCE

*" How can a man be born when he is old ? "—*JOHN III. 4.

IT has been thought by some that Nicodemus uttered these words because he was an old man. I do not think he was; old people do not travel alone in the night. Nor is the idea of personal old age implied in the question. Christ had declared the universal need for a second birth. Nicodemus says: "At that rate, all the aged unbelievers will remain unconverted. There is no hope of changing habits of thought which have become inveterate. The young may take on new ideas; but the old cannot. In order to do so, they would require to perform the impossible feat of passing through the process of birth a second time." The language of Nicodemus is not personal but sympathetic; he is not thinking of himself, but of others. Christ tells him, however, that there is no age-limit for the second birth of a soul. "The wind bloweth where it listeth; so is every one that is born of the Spirit." He says in effect: "The spirit has liberty at every age; it can sweep the woods of autumn equally with the fields of spring. The flesh has a limit of years—a limit beyond which it can renew itself no more. But the spirit can break into morning at midnight, into June in January, into foliage in the frost of winter. The lark in the soul may sing in the *evening*. The dawn in the heart may come at the closing. The joy of the life may wait for the setting. The *spirit* of a man may be raised even at the last day." That is what Jesus meant; and it is true. We speak of the burdens of age; and it has burdens. But, say as you will, there are burdens which age *removes*, and these the heaviest ones. Care presses most upon the morning, just because it is the morning. I am more troubled by shadows in hope than by shadows in memory. Earth is uncertain in my early hours; and uncertainty is unfavourable to song. But in life's evening I can sing. I have no longer to *provide* for myself. Personal outlook is ended; what remains is for God to do—not for me. It seems the true time for being young—the careless time, the free time, the spiritually unweighted time. No wonder Jacob carolled *then* with the first song of his life! No wonder he swept, in age, the harp-strings that in his youth were silent! He had no longer to provide for his youth by a stair, for his pillow by a stone, for his daybreak by a wrestling of the soul. The wings of the spirit came when the wings of the morning had rest.

Lord, give me the spirit of youth! Forbid that in my old age men should say, " He belongs to a former generation "! I want to belong to the newest generation. I want my spirit to light its torch not at yesterday's but at to-morrow's sky. I want to be numbered with the race that is coming in rather than with the race that is going out. I *can* be so numbered; my spirit can be born again when I am old. I refuse to subscribe to that moral of the fleeting years—" We all do fade as a leaf." Not as a leaf would I fade, but as a dawn. I would lose myself only in larger light. I would fade in a fuller radiance, I would merge in a mightier stream. If my taper expire, let it be in tints of gold! Kindle me again at the fire of the new generation! Let my heart catch the glow of the coming sun! However old my flesh may be, let my sympathies be young! Write my name among the early sons of this century! Interest me in their problems; inspire me with their aims; inflame me with their larger view! Give me fellowship with the love-feast of Cana; let not romance be rusted by life's afternoon! Give me sympathy with the hour of first temptation; remind me of life's primitive hunger! Give me tenderness for youth's aspirings; let me stand on its mount of beatitudes and see its coming kingdom! Give me kindliness even to early presumption; let me forgive James and John for underrating the depth of the cup! The climax of Thy leading is to make me young when I am old.

THE MORAL TAUGHT BY THE IDLE THESSALONIANS

"We hear that there are some which walk among you disorderly, working not at all."—2 THES. III. 11.

THE disorderliness here spoken of was the result not of religious unbelief but of religious conviction. These Thessalonians refused to work on earth because they looked for an immediate advent of heaven. Christ was coming; He might be expected any hour of any day. What was the use of beginning work which might be interrupted ere it was half done! Why start the building of a house when there was imminent expectation of a house not made with hands! Why launch a ship for the voyage when the time was about to come in which there should be no more sea! Why teach the boy at school when tongues were about to cease and knowledge to vanish away! Why study human politics when the kingdoms of this world were to become the kingdom of the Lord and of His Christ! So asked the Thessalonian workmen; and in answer they folded

284

their hands in rest. They deemed it a waste of time to labour at structures which might ere long be superseded. It was to counteract such a spirit that Paul wrote this epistle. It is to my mind the most peculiar writing in the Bible. It is the only book of Scripture I know which is written with the express design of moderating the sense of another world. Paul seeks to throw a veil over the coming of Christ. He feels that the Thessalonians have too near a view of heaven—a view so near that it makes them unpractical towards the earth. He restores their practicalness by shrouding their vision—by bringing a cloud over the transfiguration glory. And truly we have all a lesson to learn here. There is nothing of which we complain so persistently as the silence of God. Here the silence of God is made a form of His benevolence—a thing necessary for the perpetuation of the world. We are shown the picture of an earth arrested by the overwhelming prominence of heaven. We are made to see what would be the effect of a letter from the sky telling that the time was brief. It might stimulate the missionary, it might benefit the evangelist; but to every other profession it would be paralysis. It would disband the army and navy. It would impoverish the lawyer. It would dull the trade

285

of the merchant. It would arrest authorship. It would stop education. It would impede the wings of medical science. It would give a quietus to philanthropy. It would cause to seem superfluous the help of man to man.

Therefore, O Lord, I thank Thee for the cloud that mingles with my sunshine. I thank Thee that there is a mist on the other side of the river. I have often lamented that the opposite bank is not more luminous; but I have changed my mind. I should not care to beautify the bank on which I dwell if I saw the other side too clearly. I often bless Thee for Thy revelations; do I sufficiently bless Thee for Thy silences? But for Thy silence I should have no speech. Should I ever provide for my children if Thy provision were made plain? Should I ever clothe the poor if I saw Thy hand weaving their garments? Should I ever redeem the lapsed if I beheld Thine angels streaming forth to save them? My efforts would be ended; my love would be lost; my charity would be chilled; my pity would be plucked up by the roots. What Thou cravest is not provision but my providing. It is to *my* care Thou hast entrusted my brother. It is to teach me my responsibility that Thou hast kept silence. If I heard the heavenly music, I should relax my toil.

286

The Moral Taught by the Idle Thessalonians

It is the mist that moves me; it is the need that nerves me; it is the doubt that dedicates me; it is the peril that prompts me; it is the unseenness that stimulates me. I have gained more by Thy silence than by Thy song. Thy song gives me faith and hope, but Thy silence teaches me charity; for it is the uncertainty of life that sends me to the help of my brother, and it is the mystery of to-morrow that wakes my sympathy with man.

BRADBURY, AGNEW, & CO. LD., PRINTERS, LONDON AND TONBRIDGE.

CPSIA information can be obtained
at www.ICGtesting.com
Printed in the USA
LVHW100952221220
674870LV00028B/239

9 781149 213766